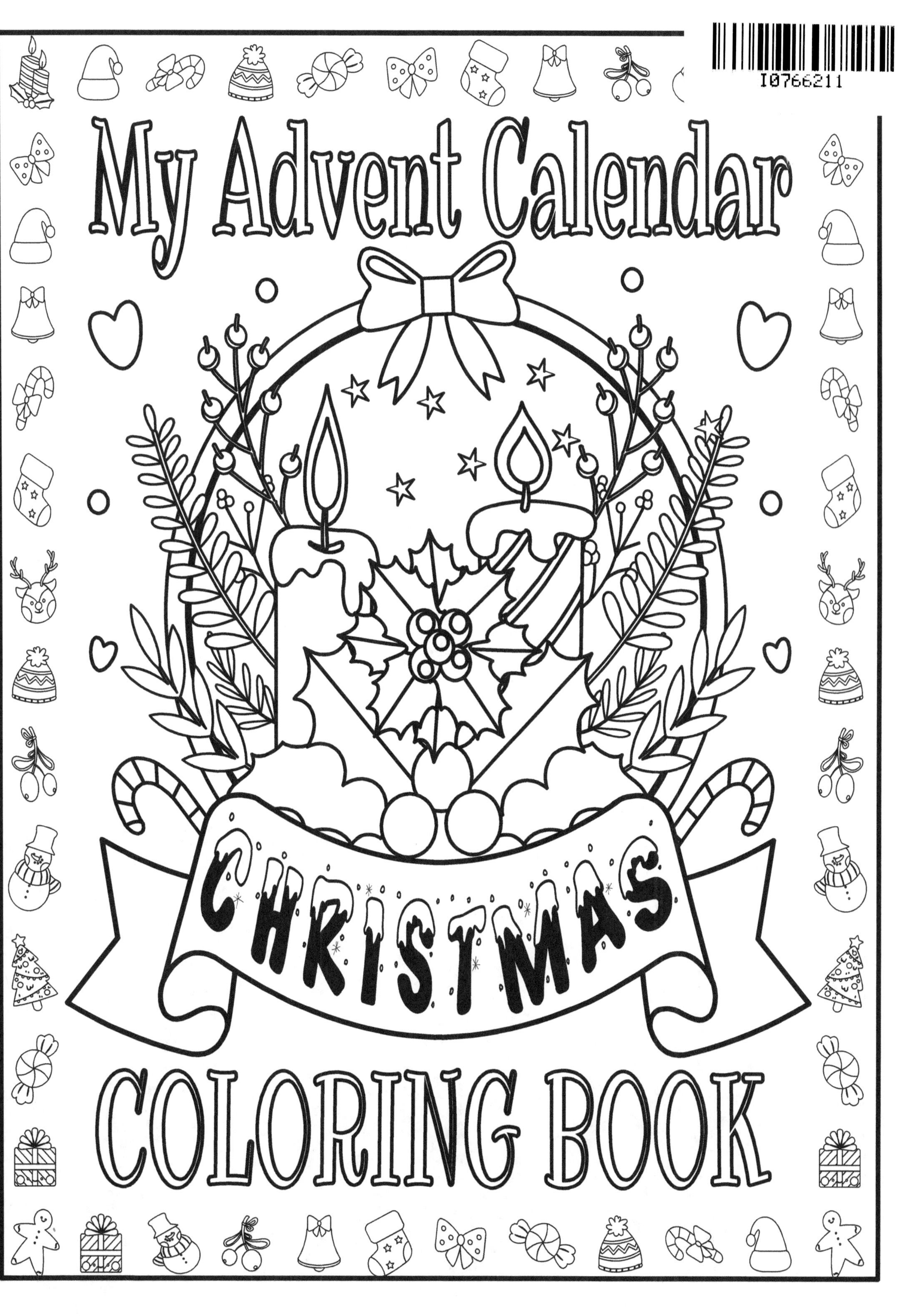
My Advent Calendar
CHRISTMAS
COLORING BOOK

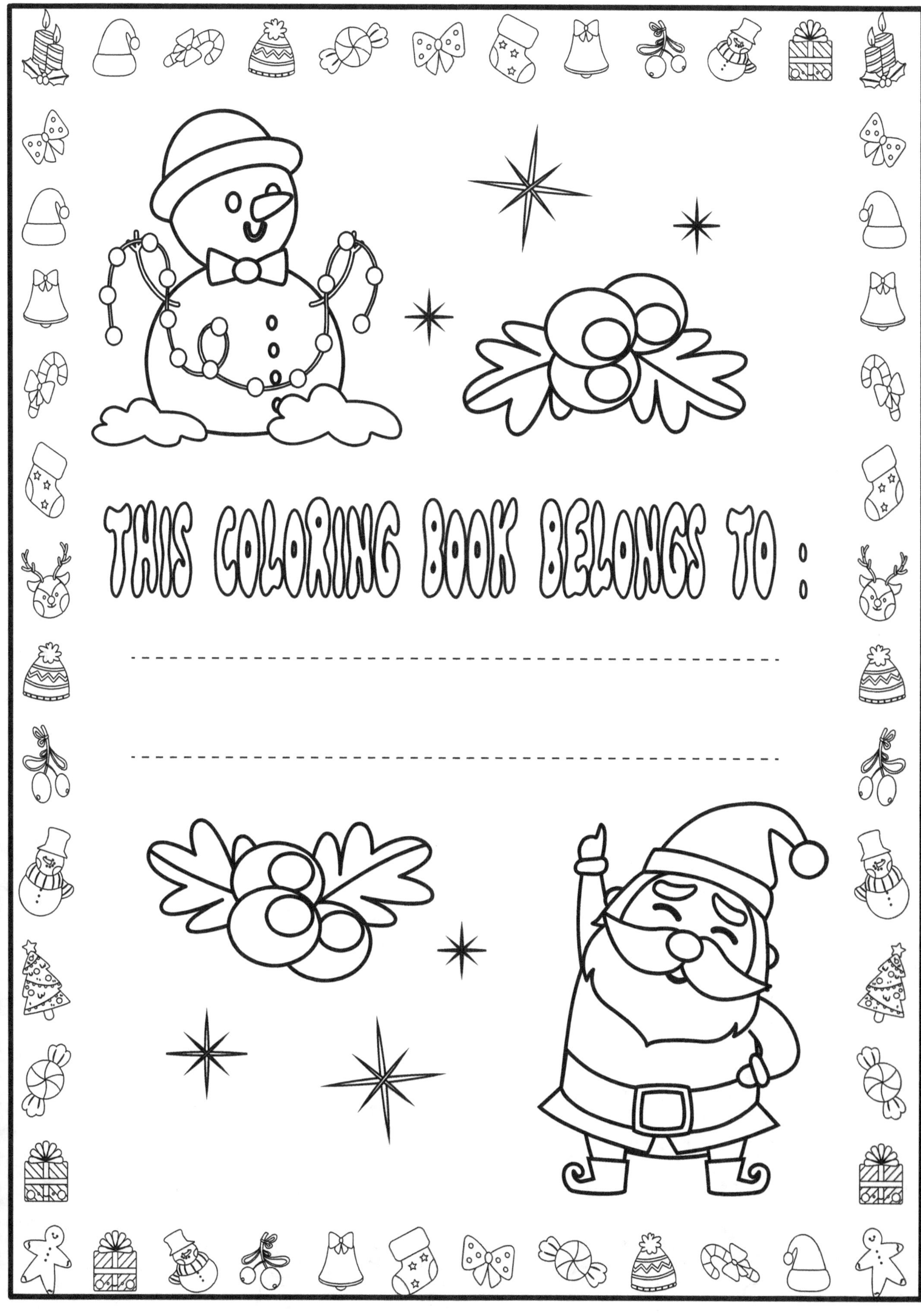
THIS COLORING BOOK BELONGS TO :

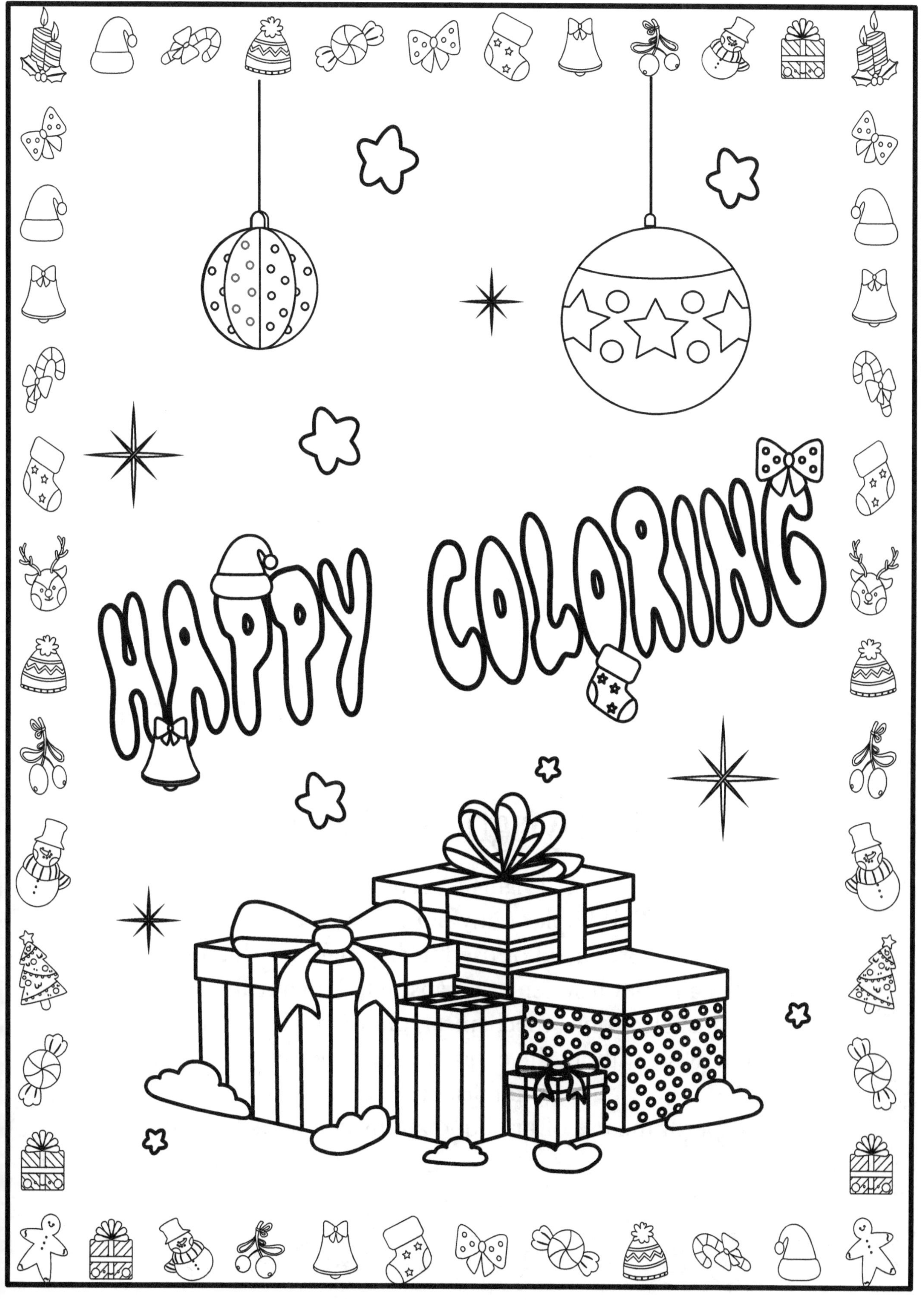
HAPPY COLORING

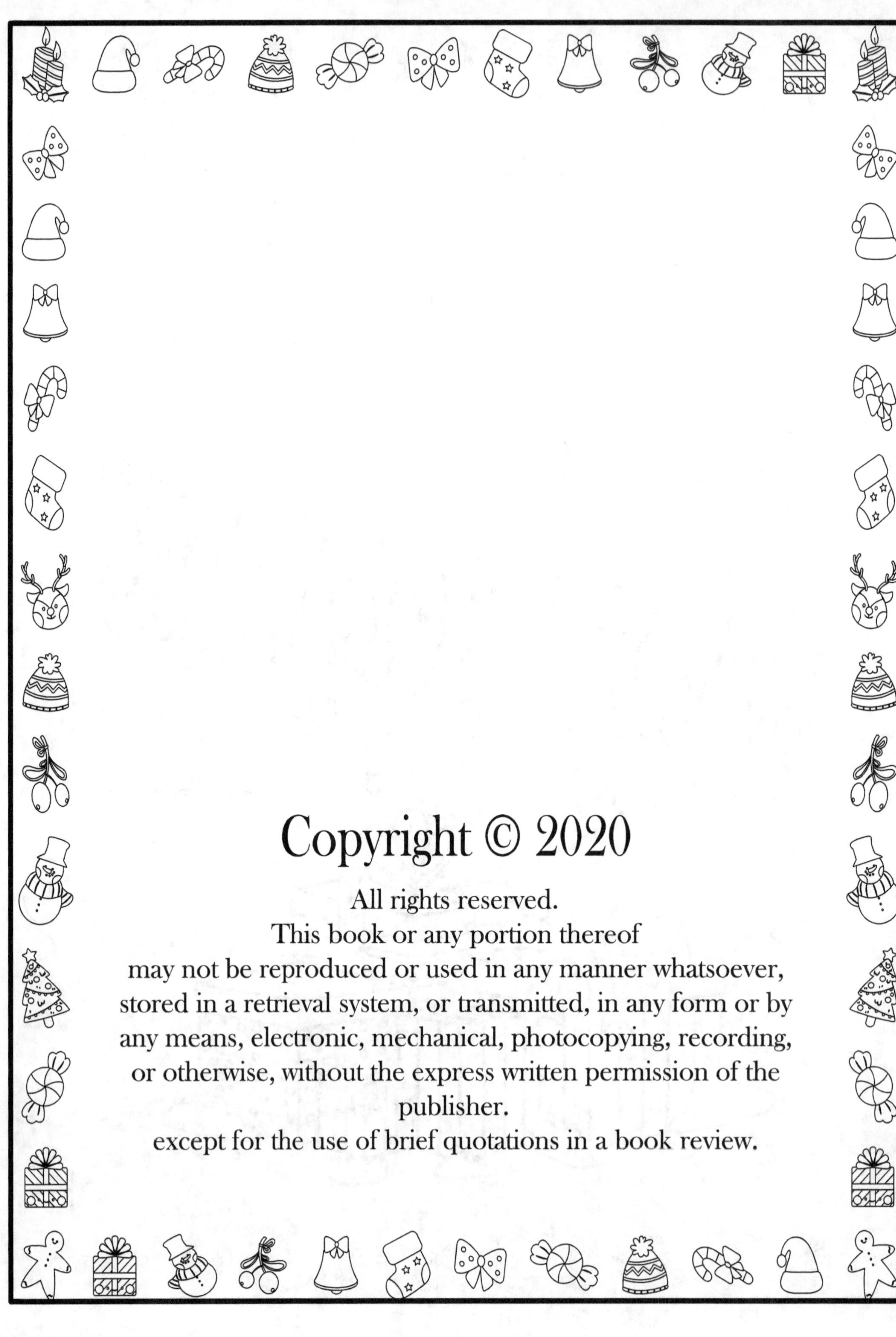

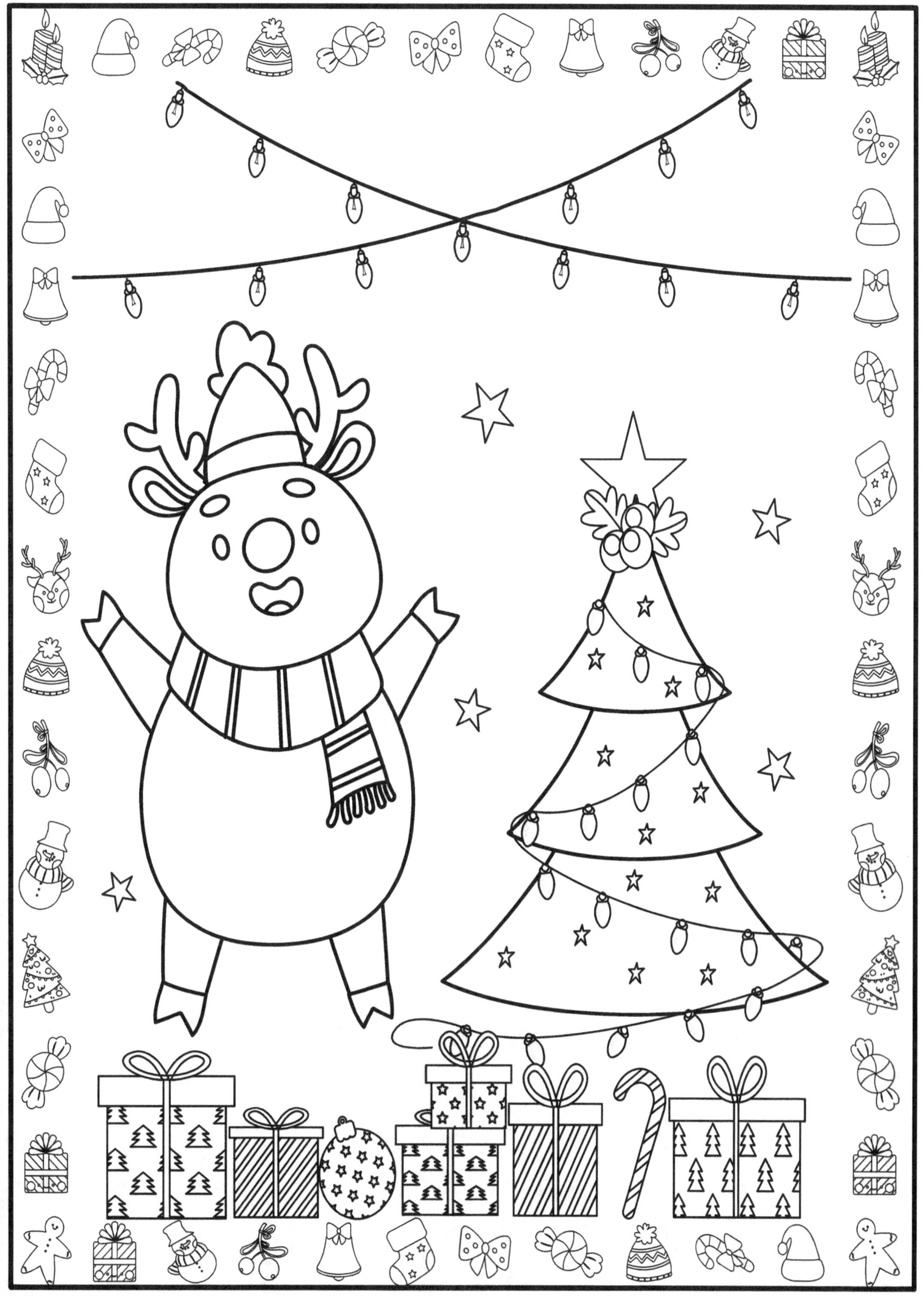

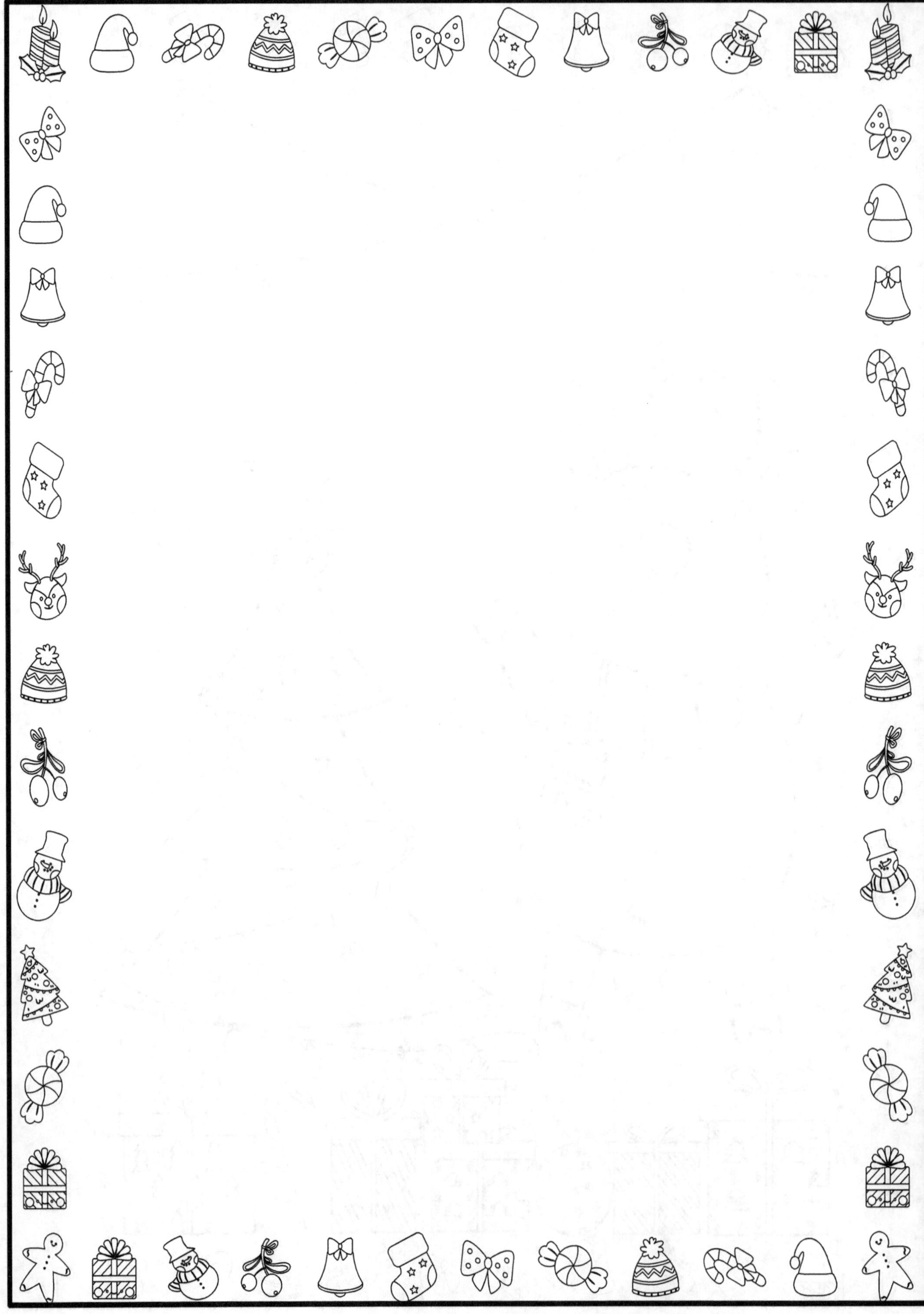

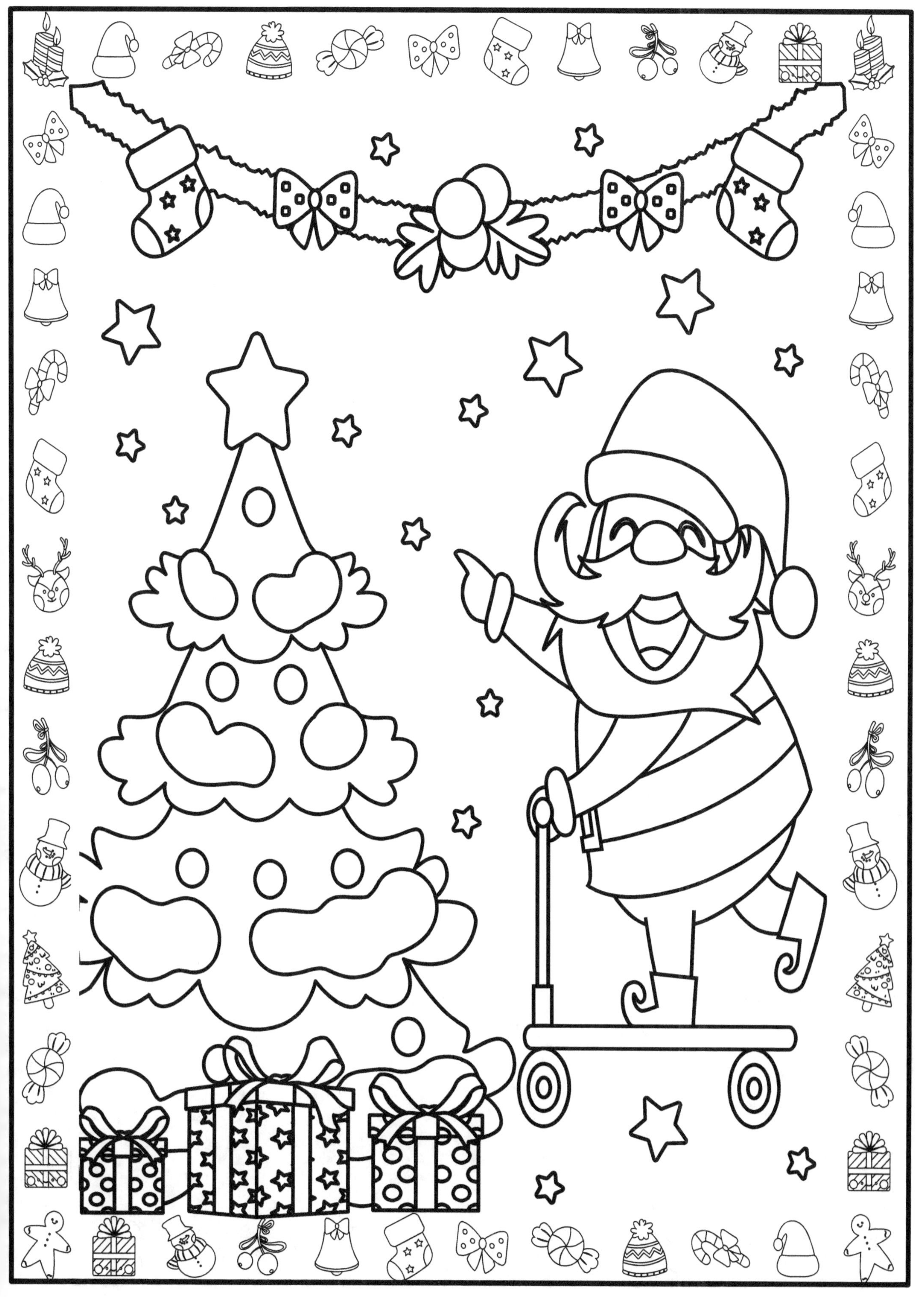

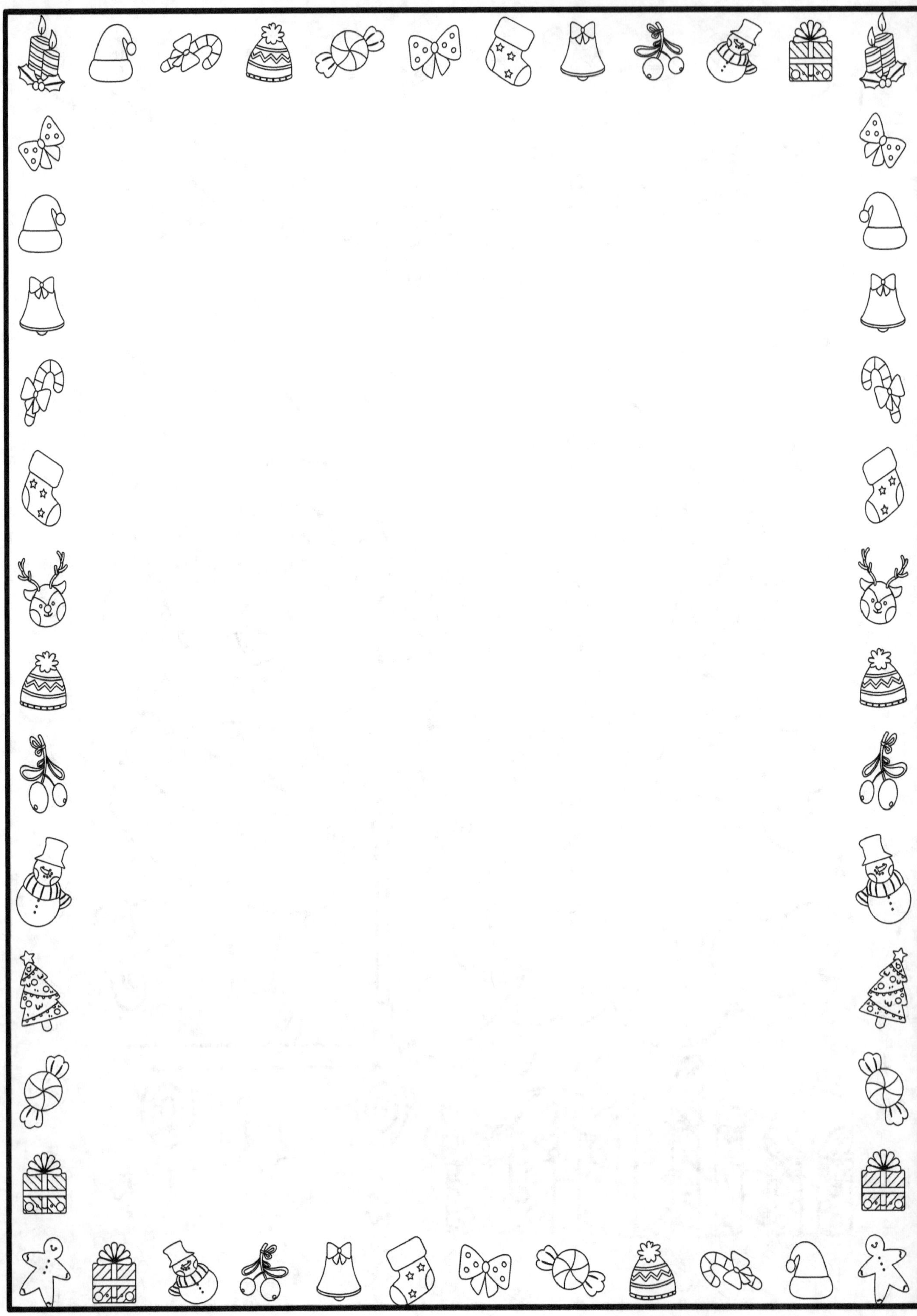

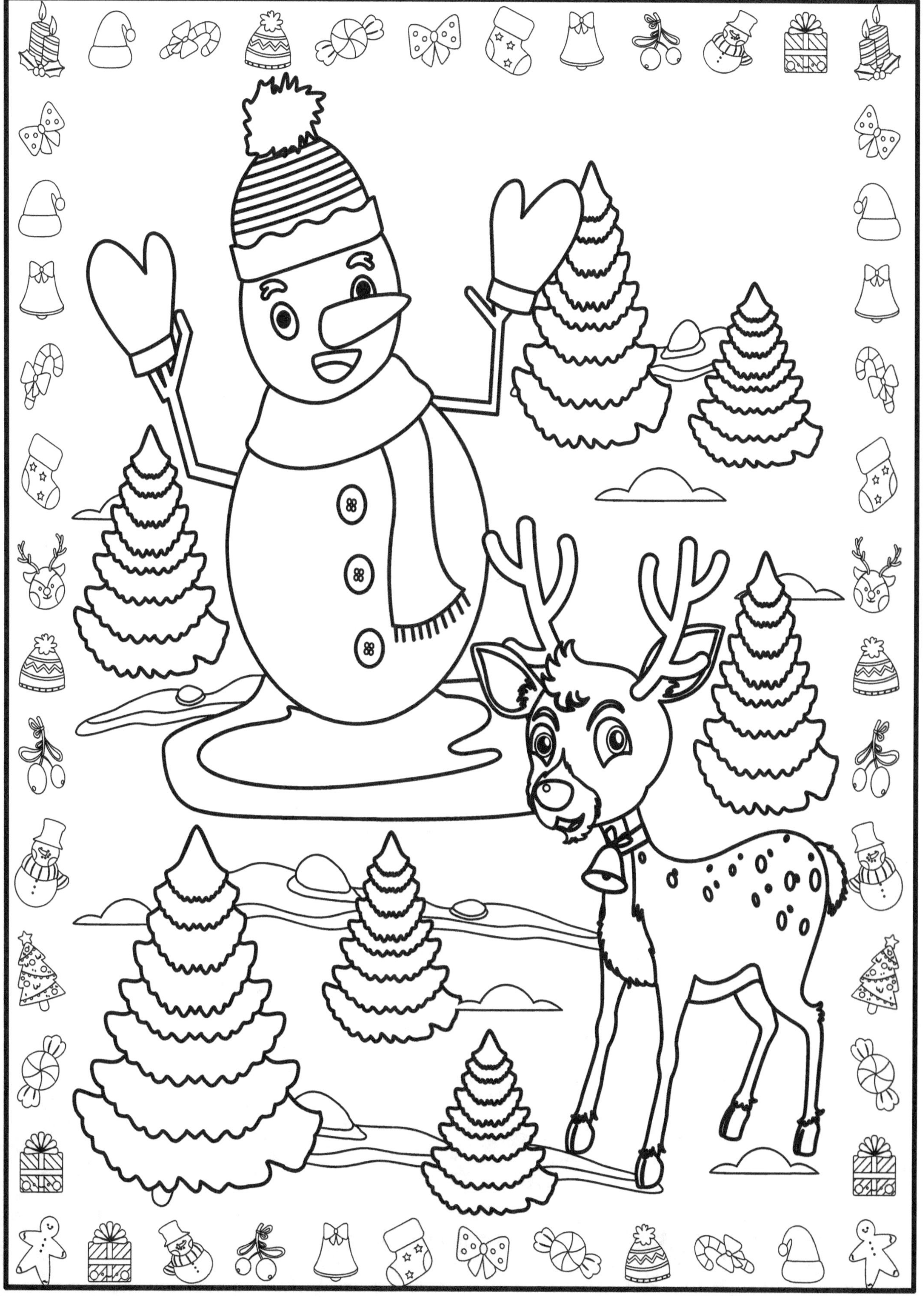

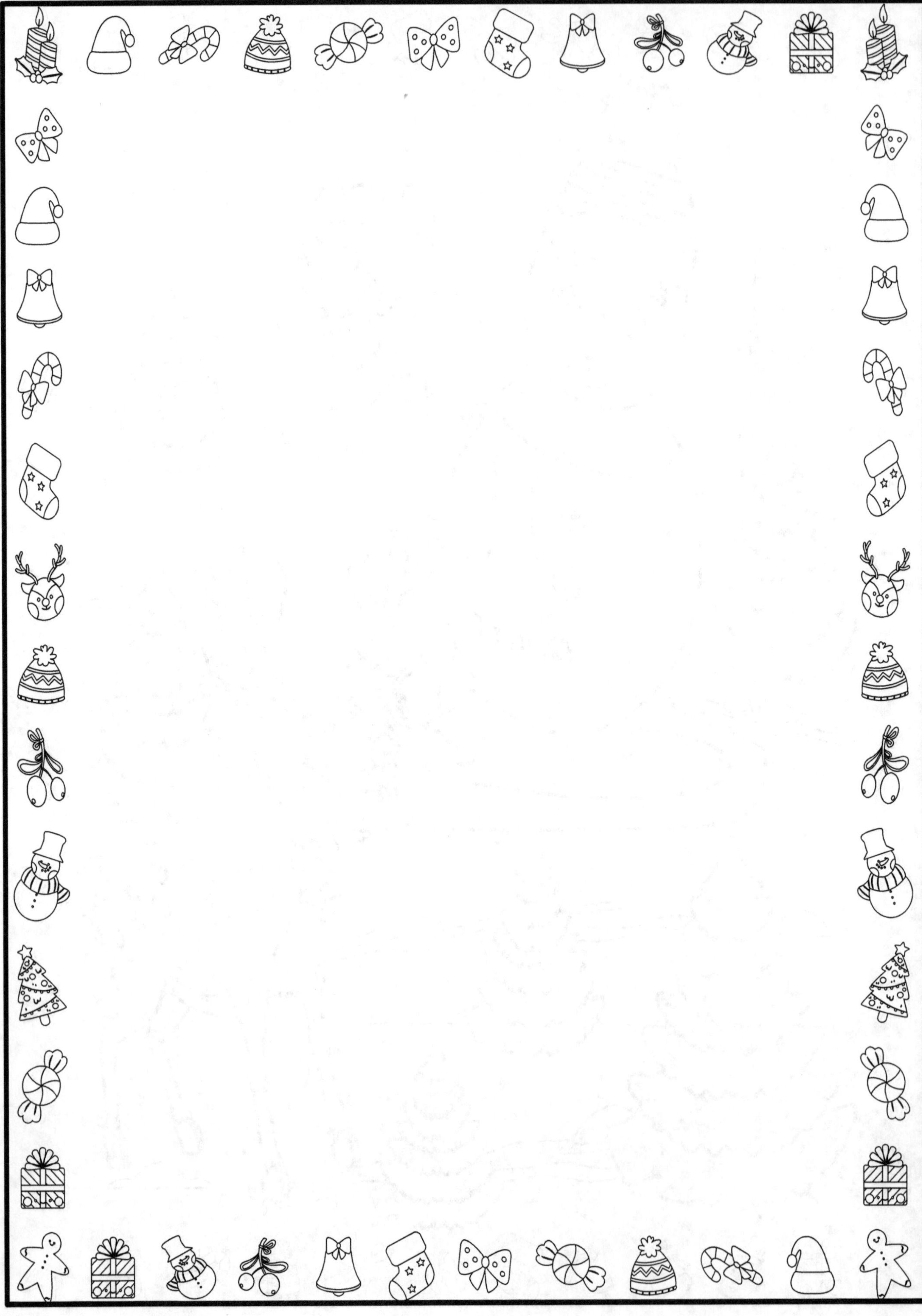

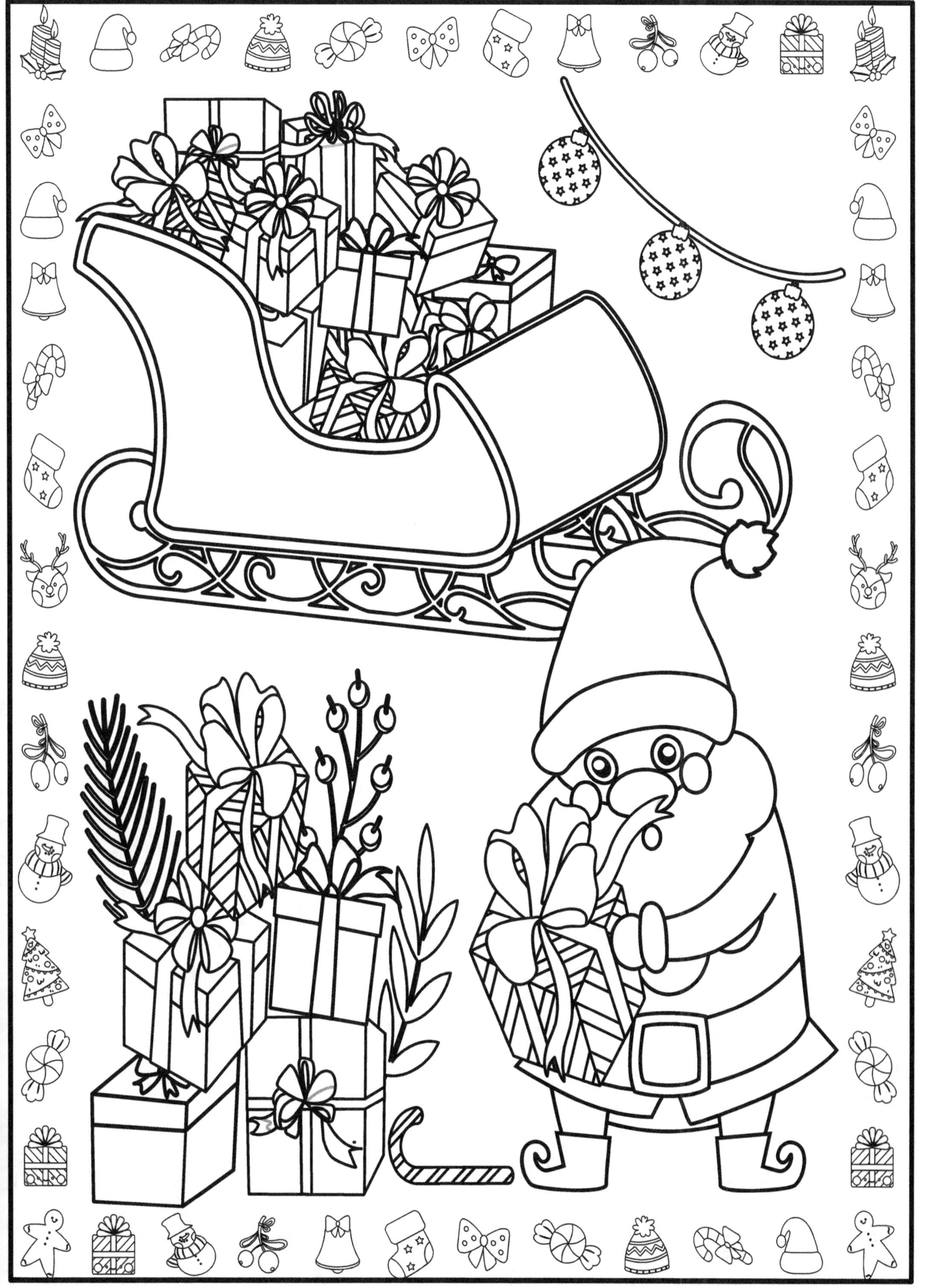

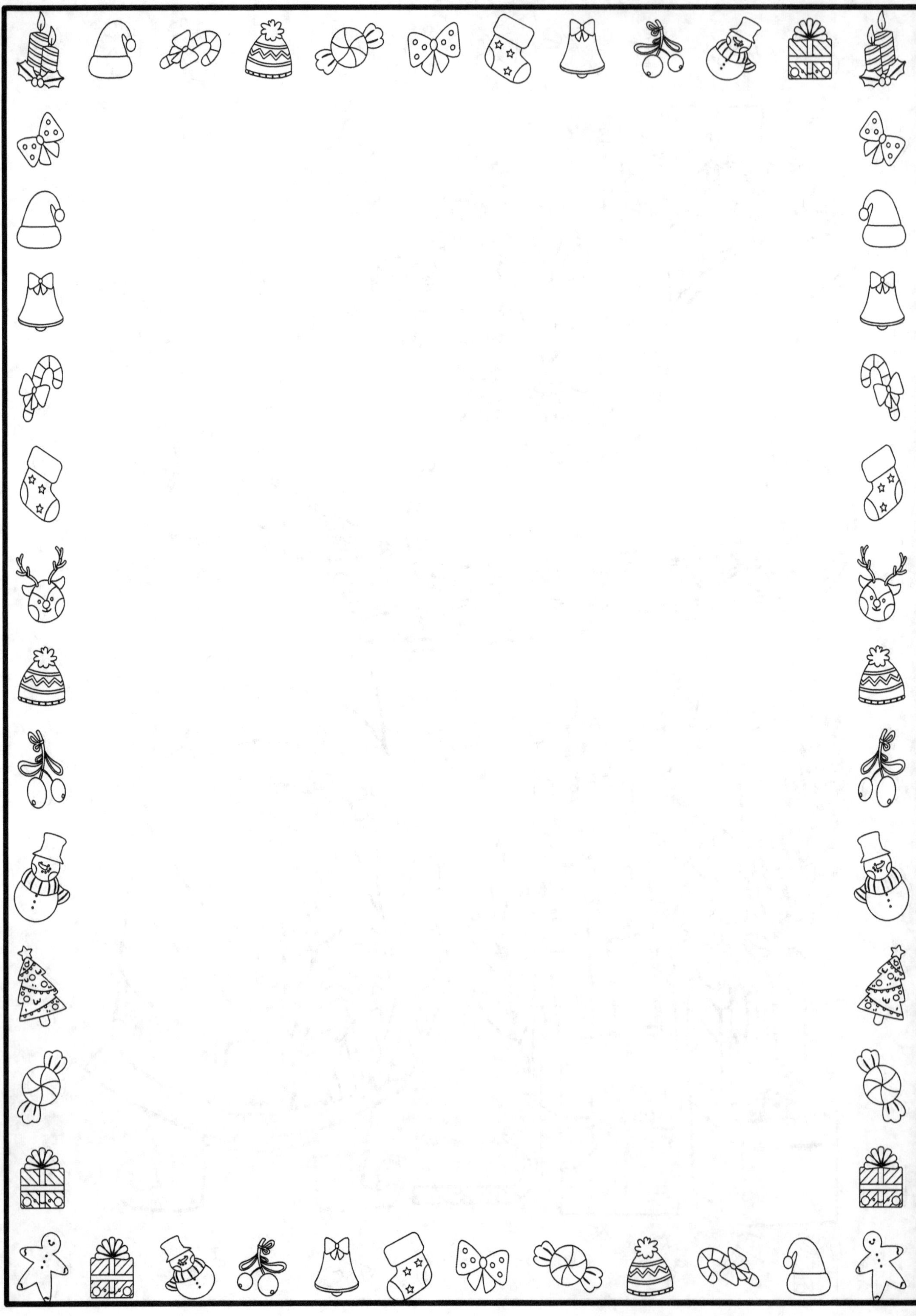

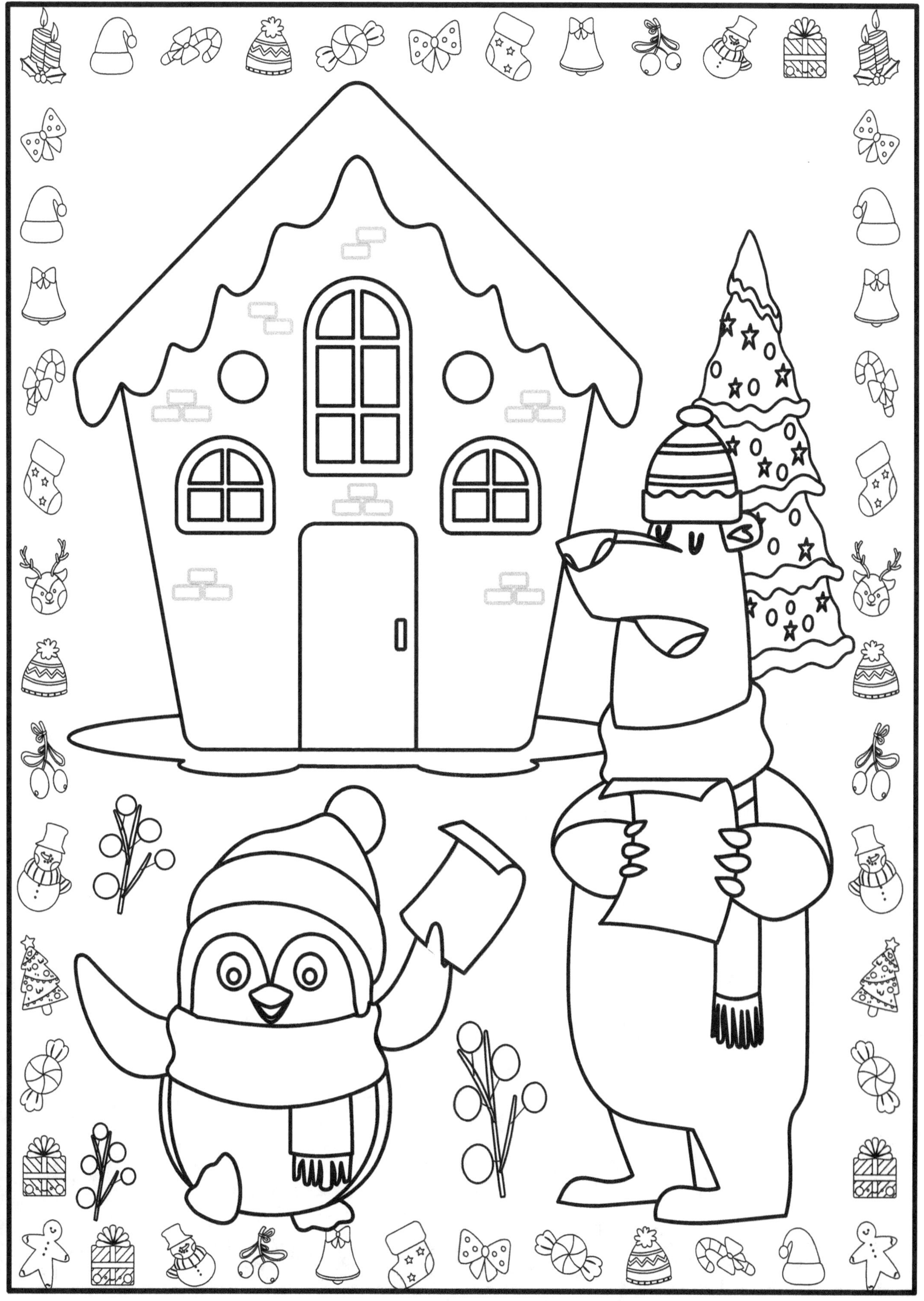

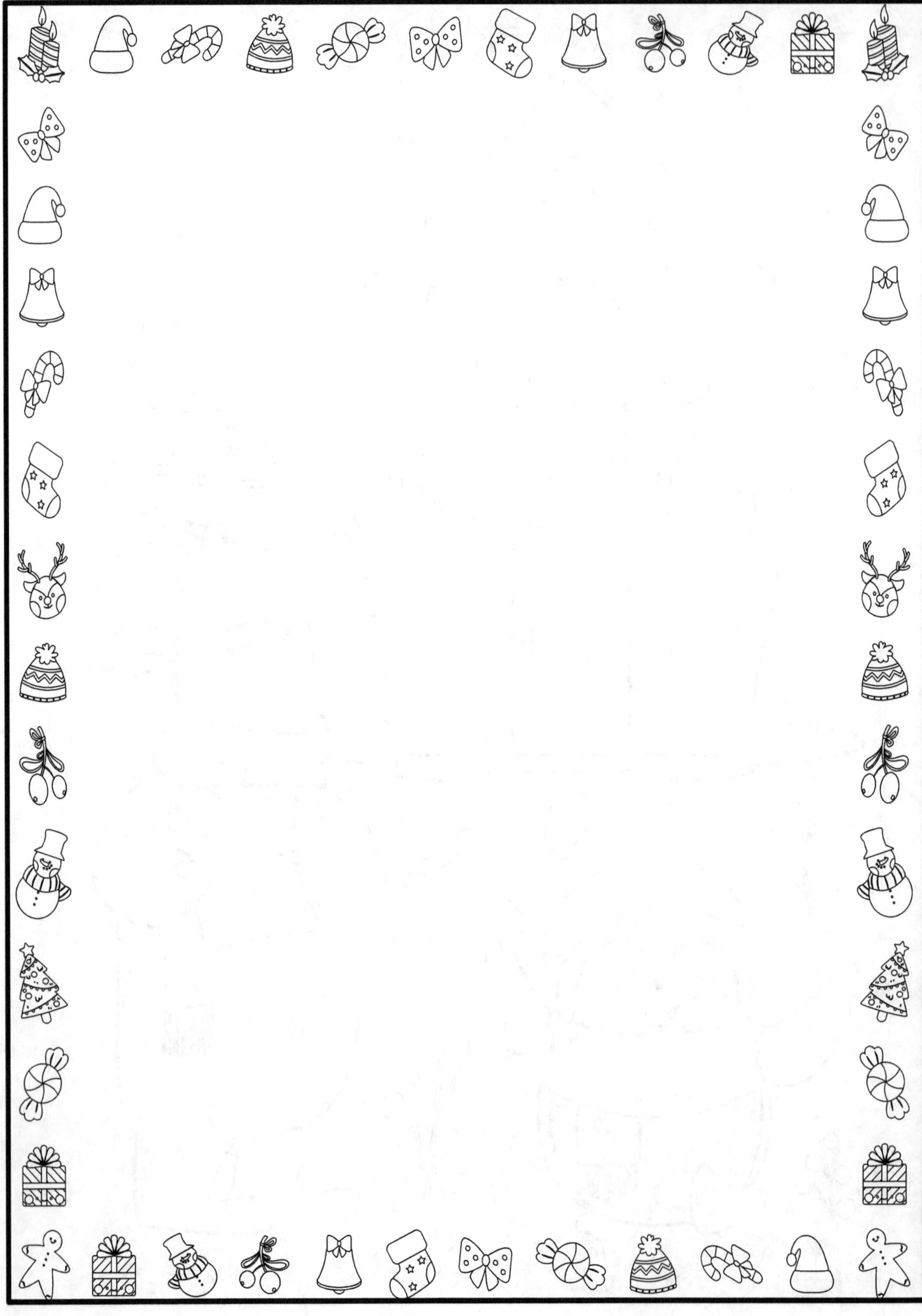

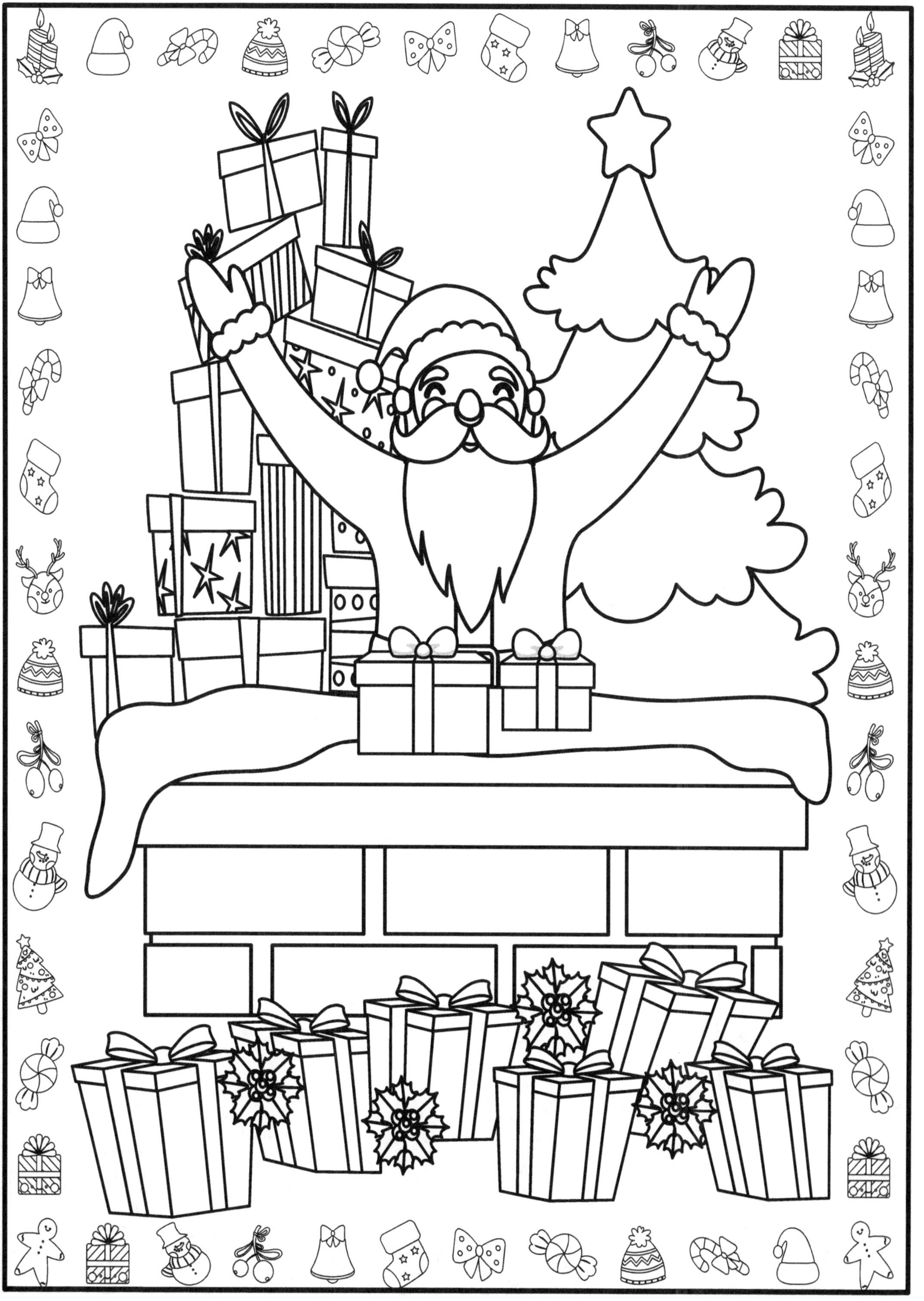

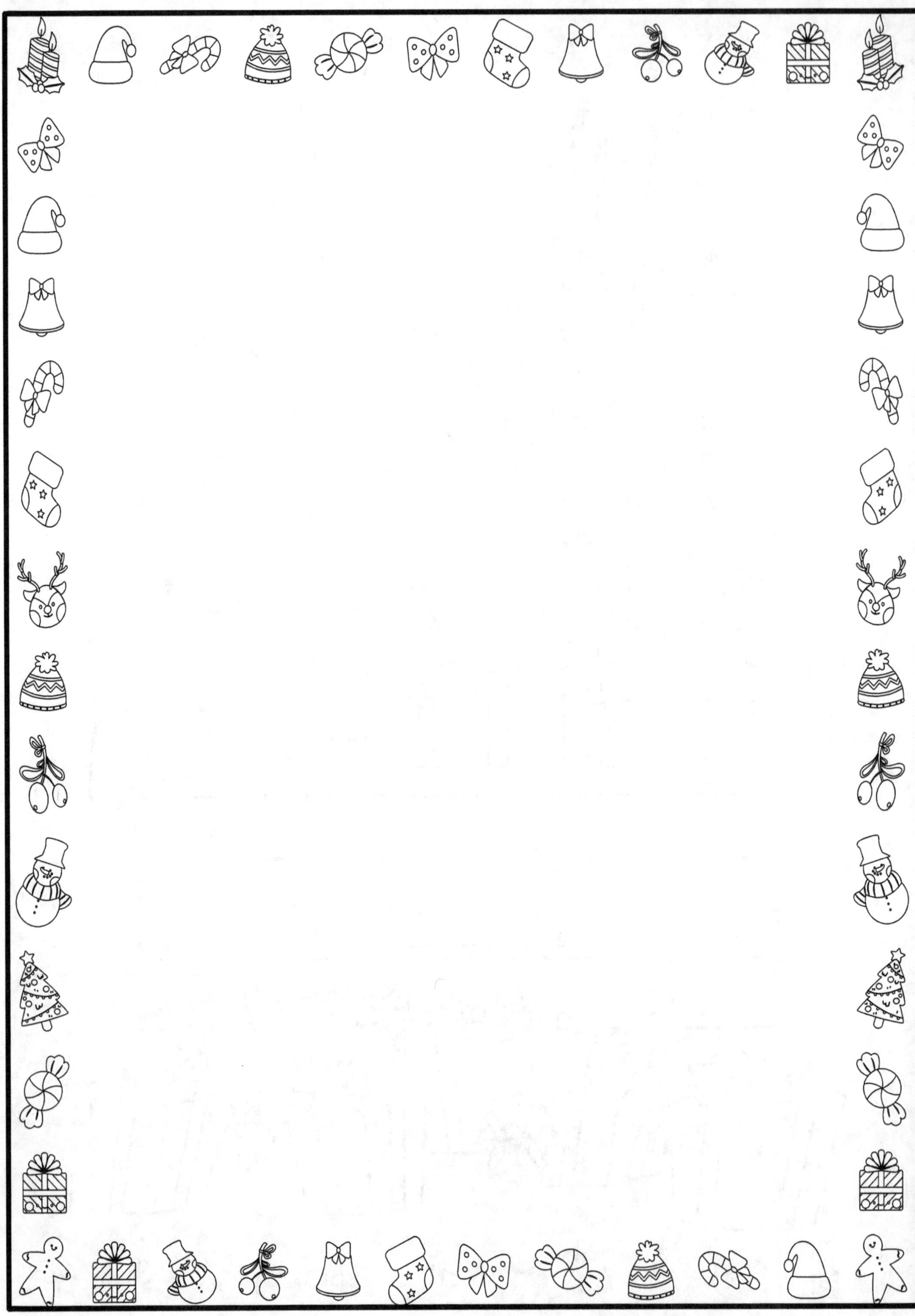

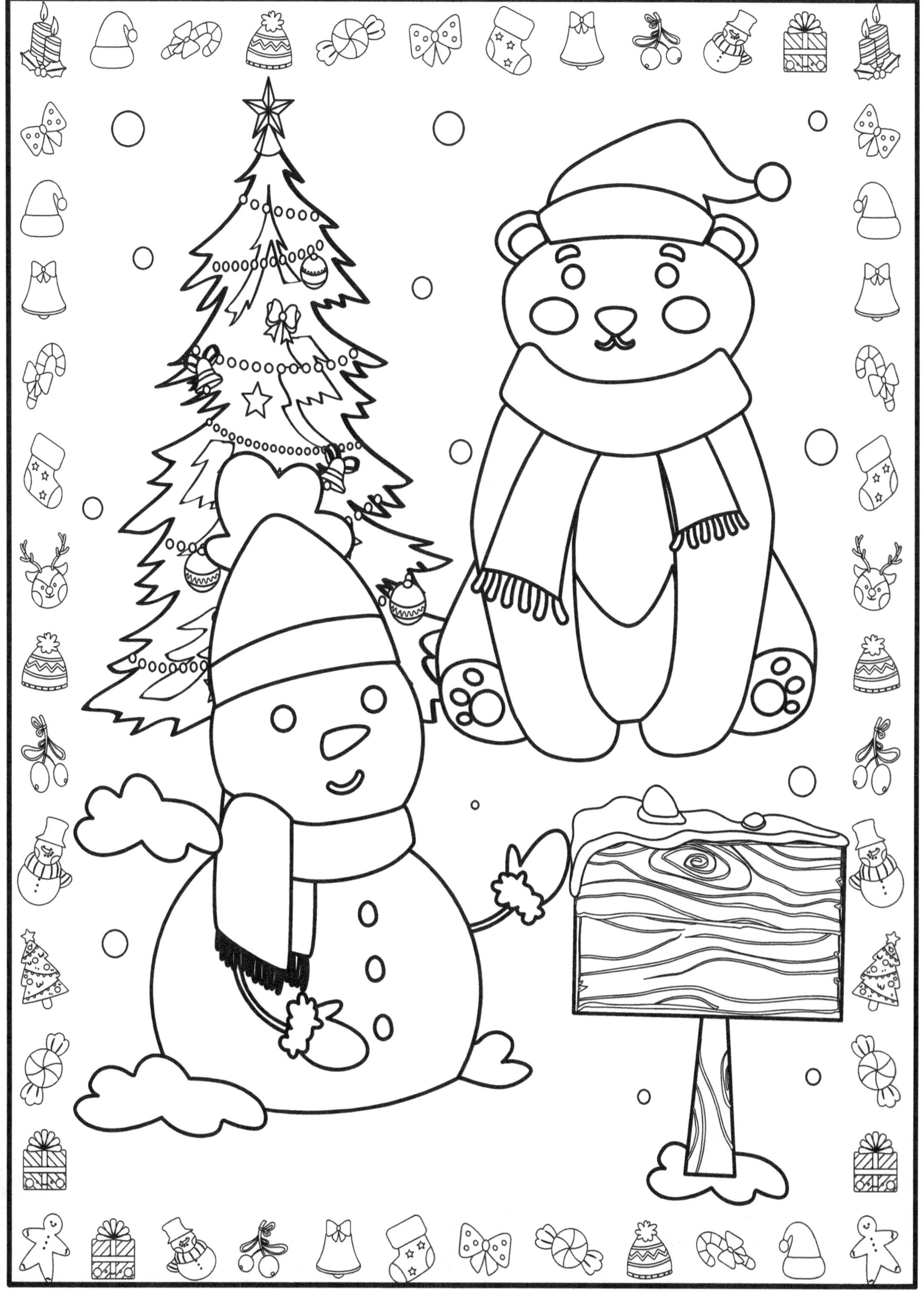

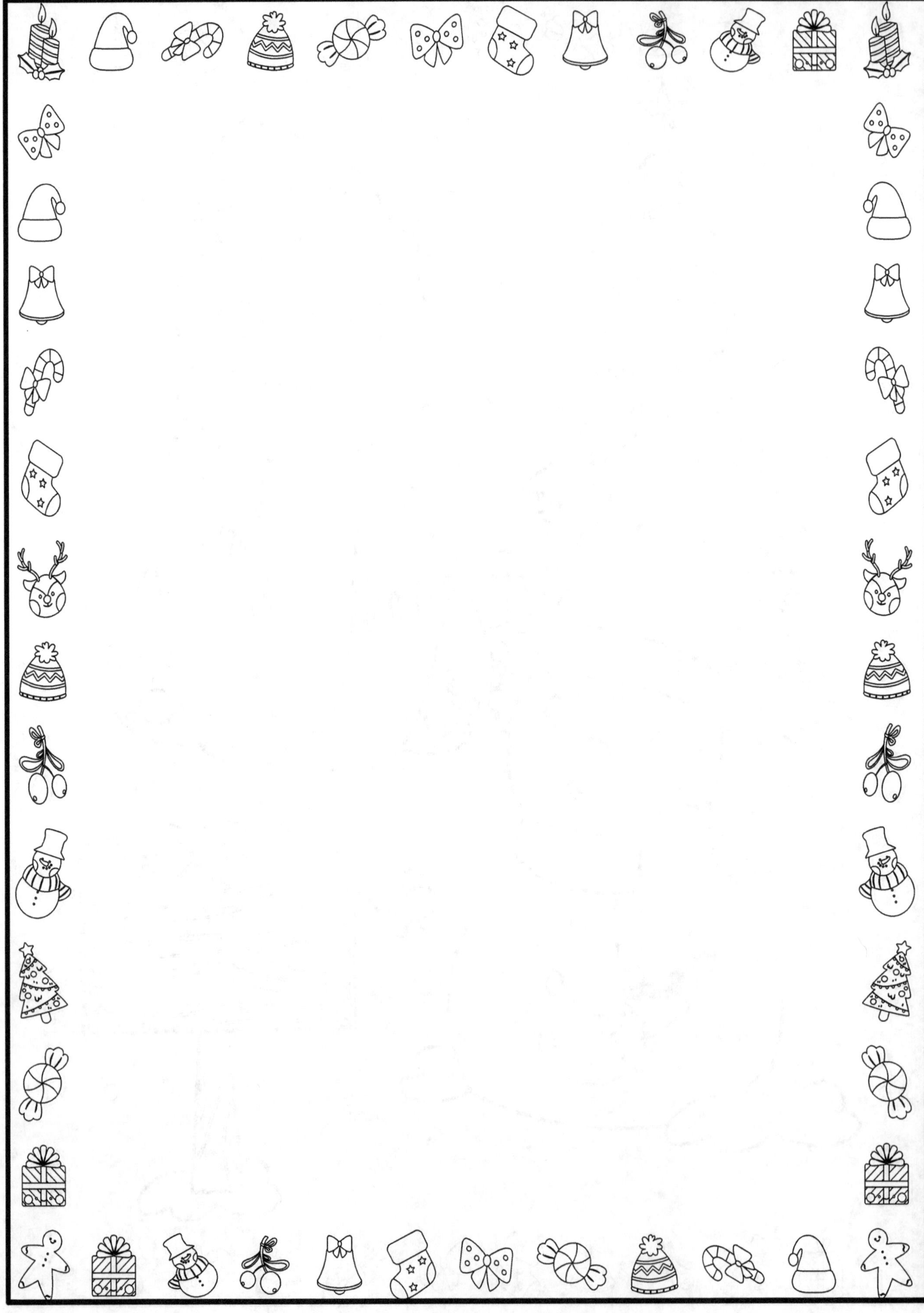

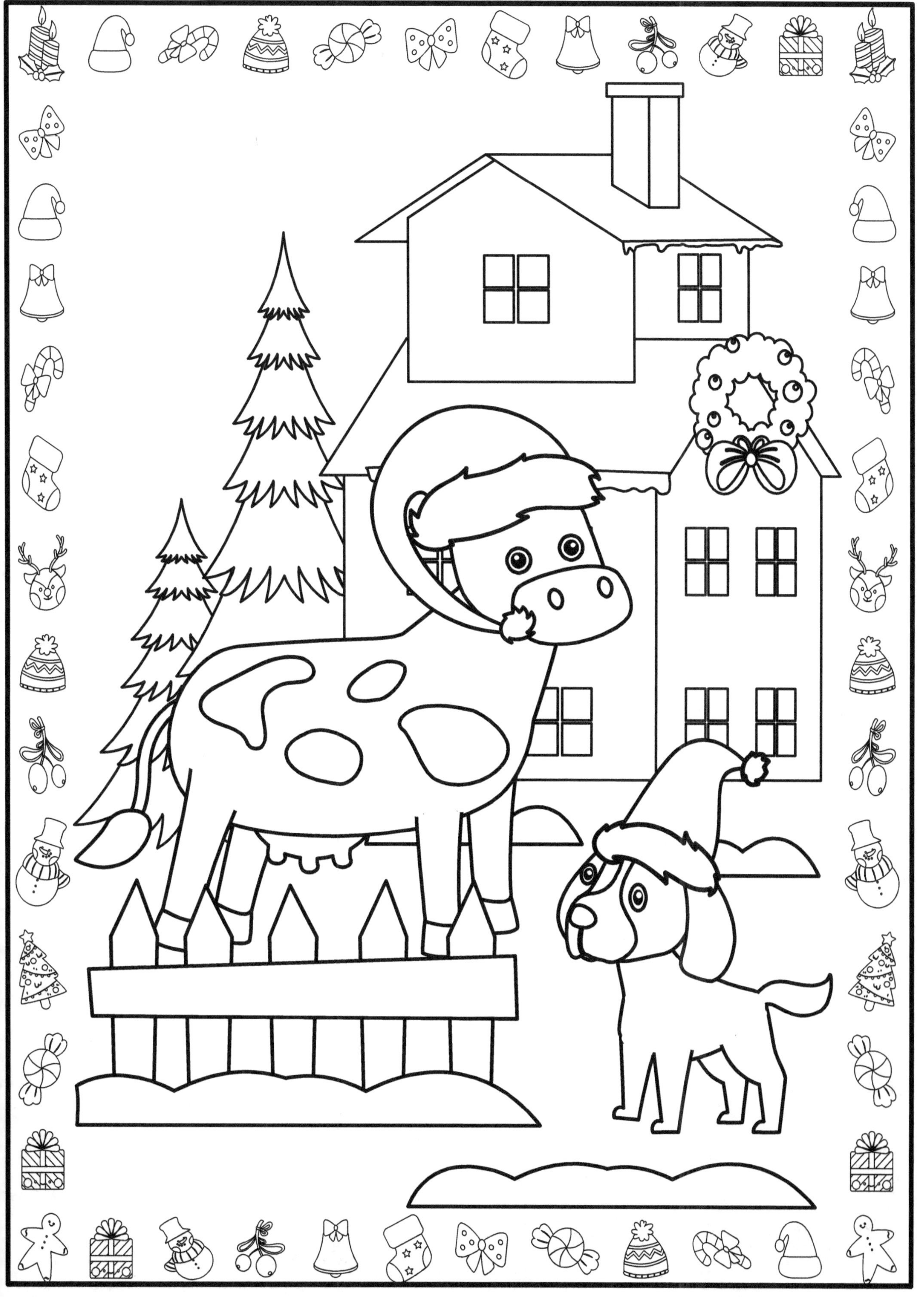

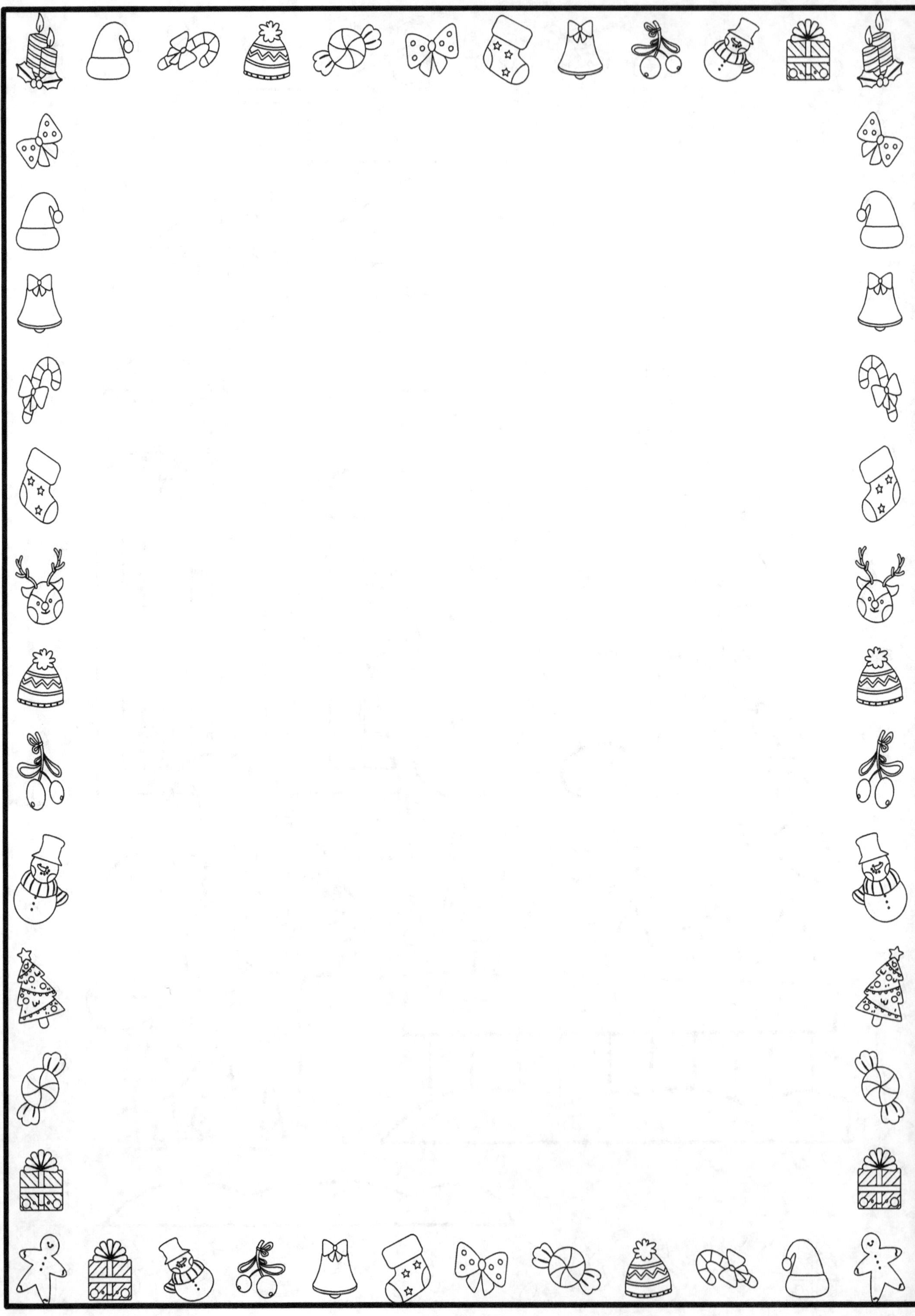

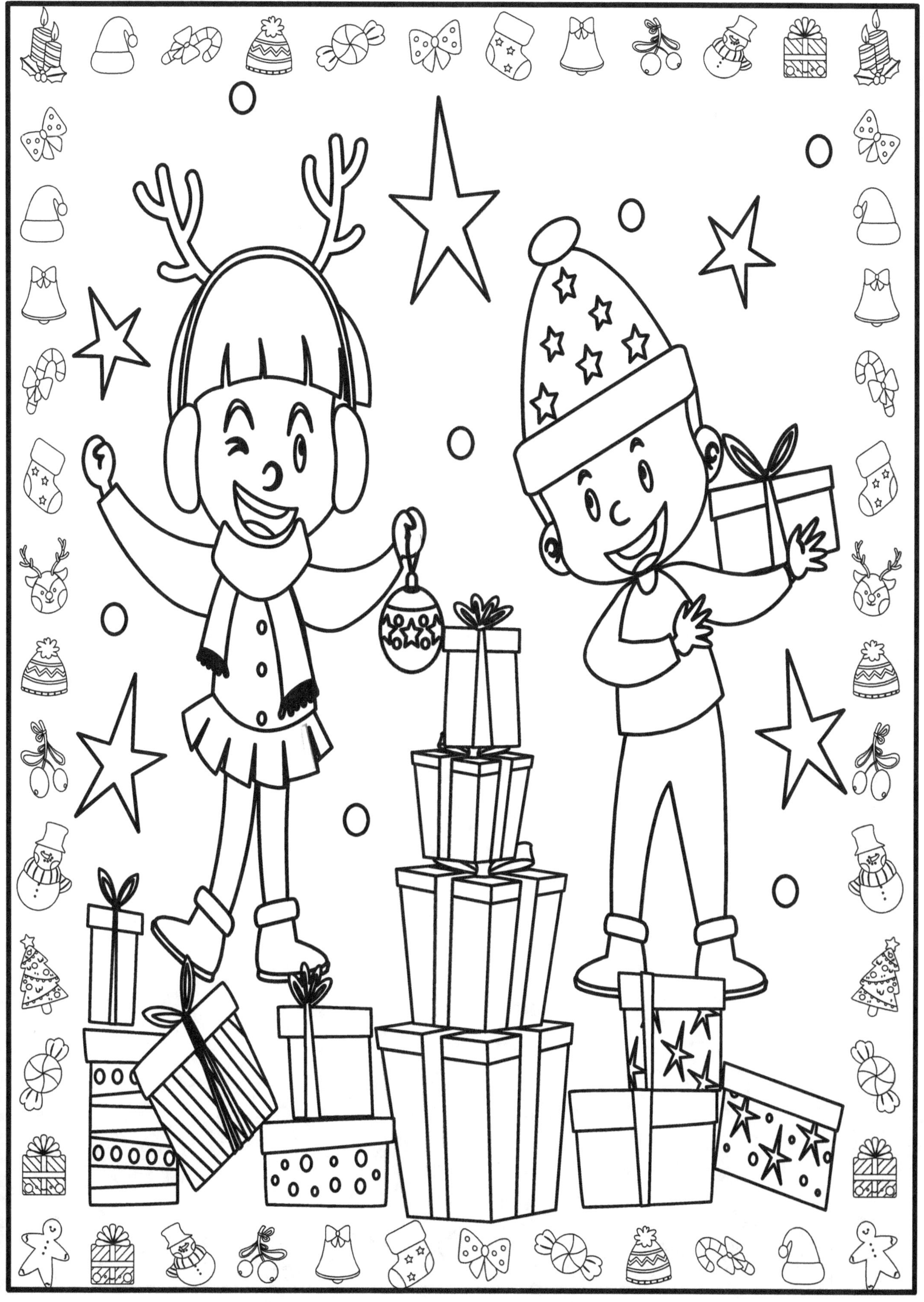

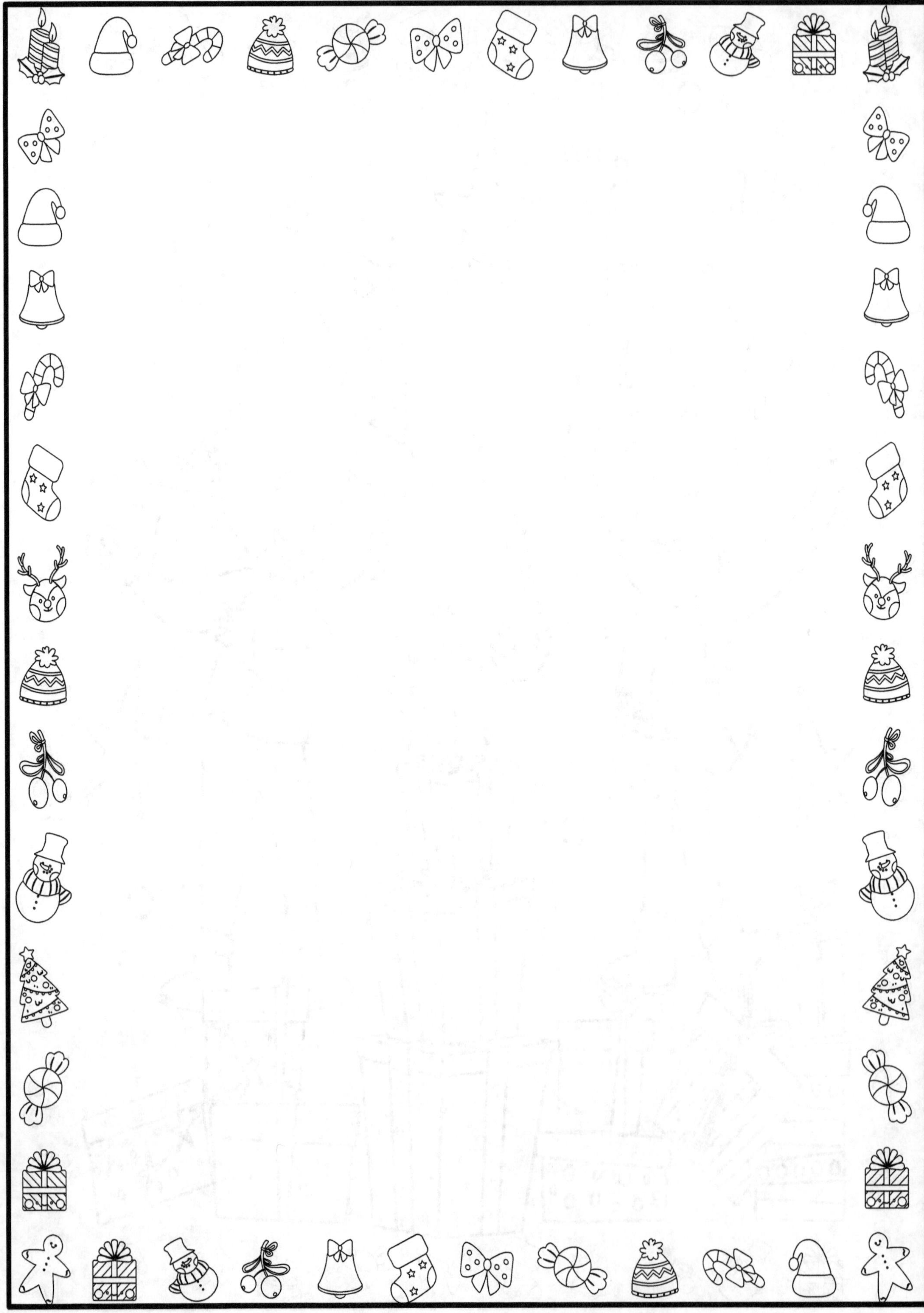

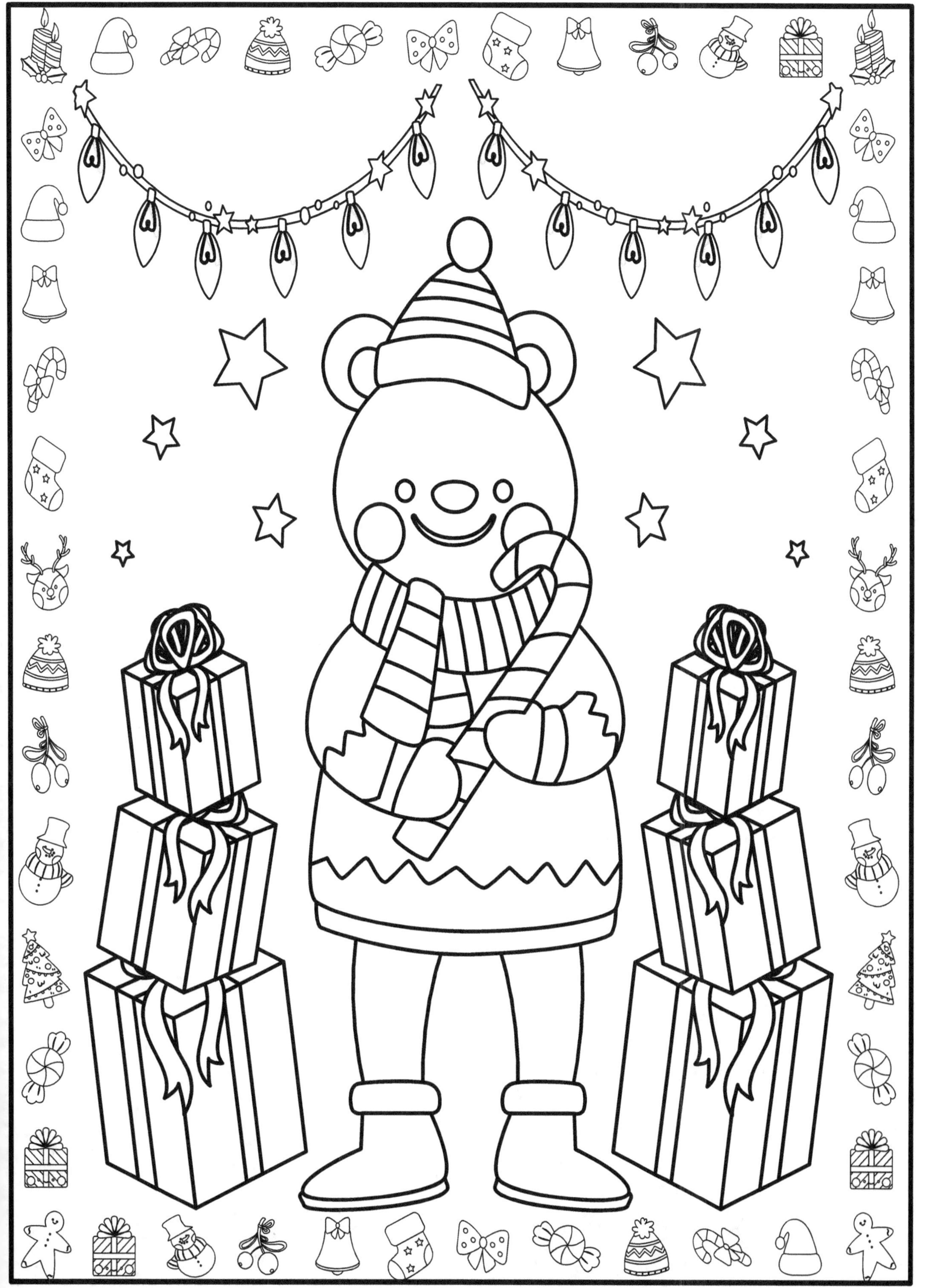

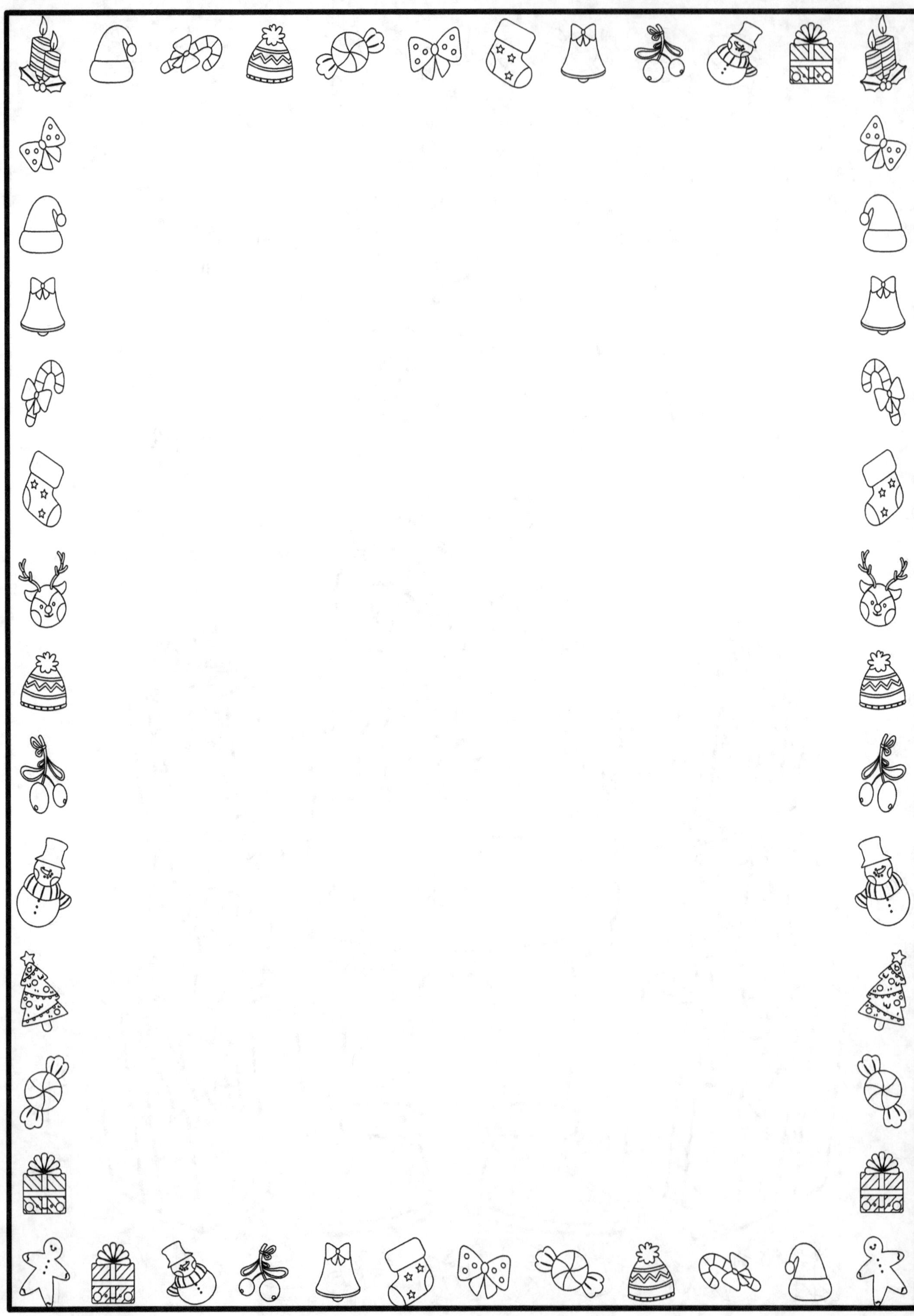

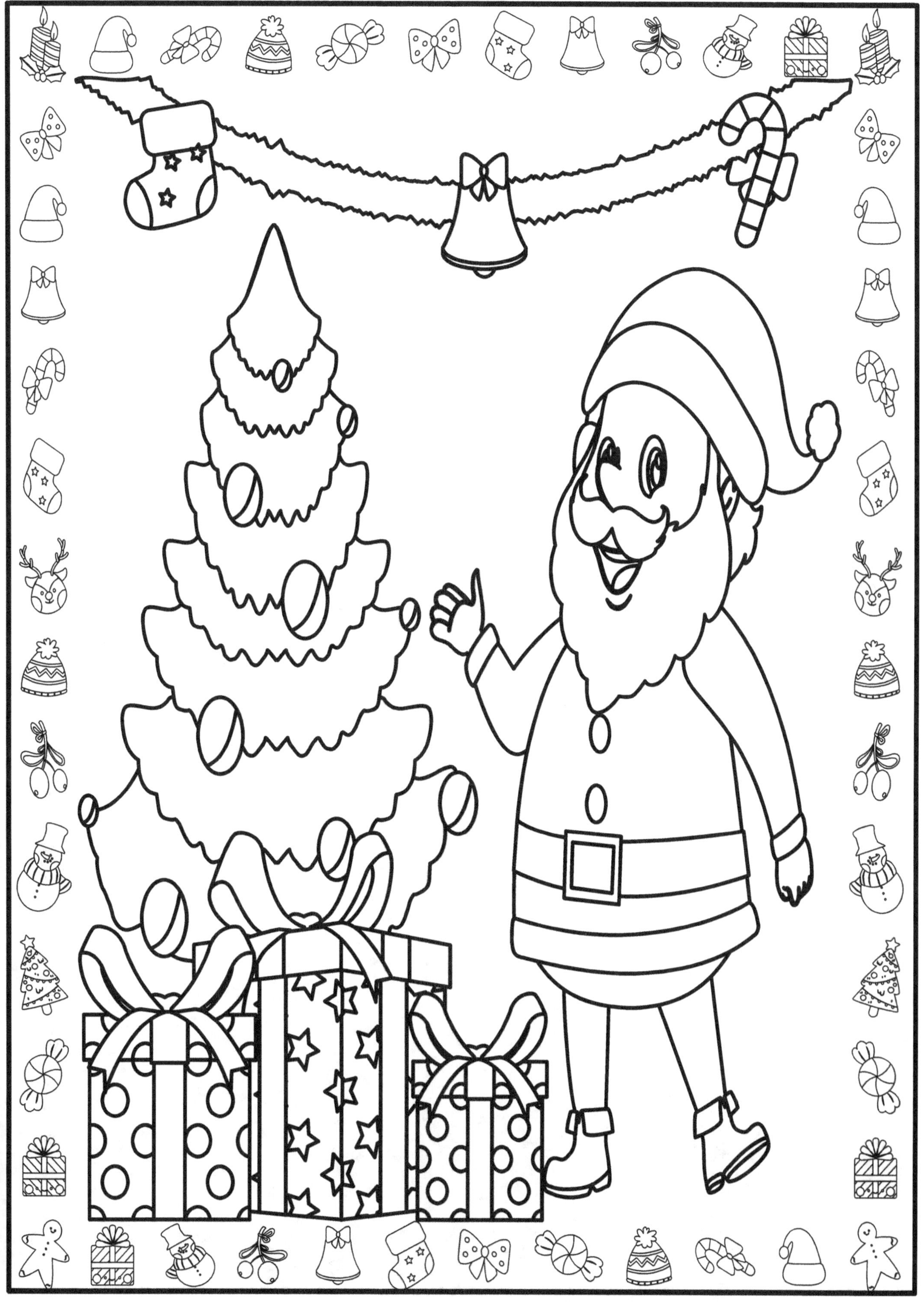

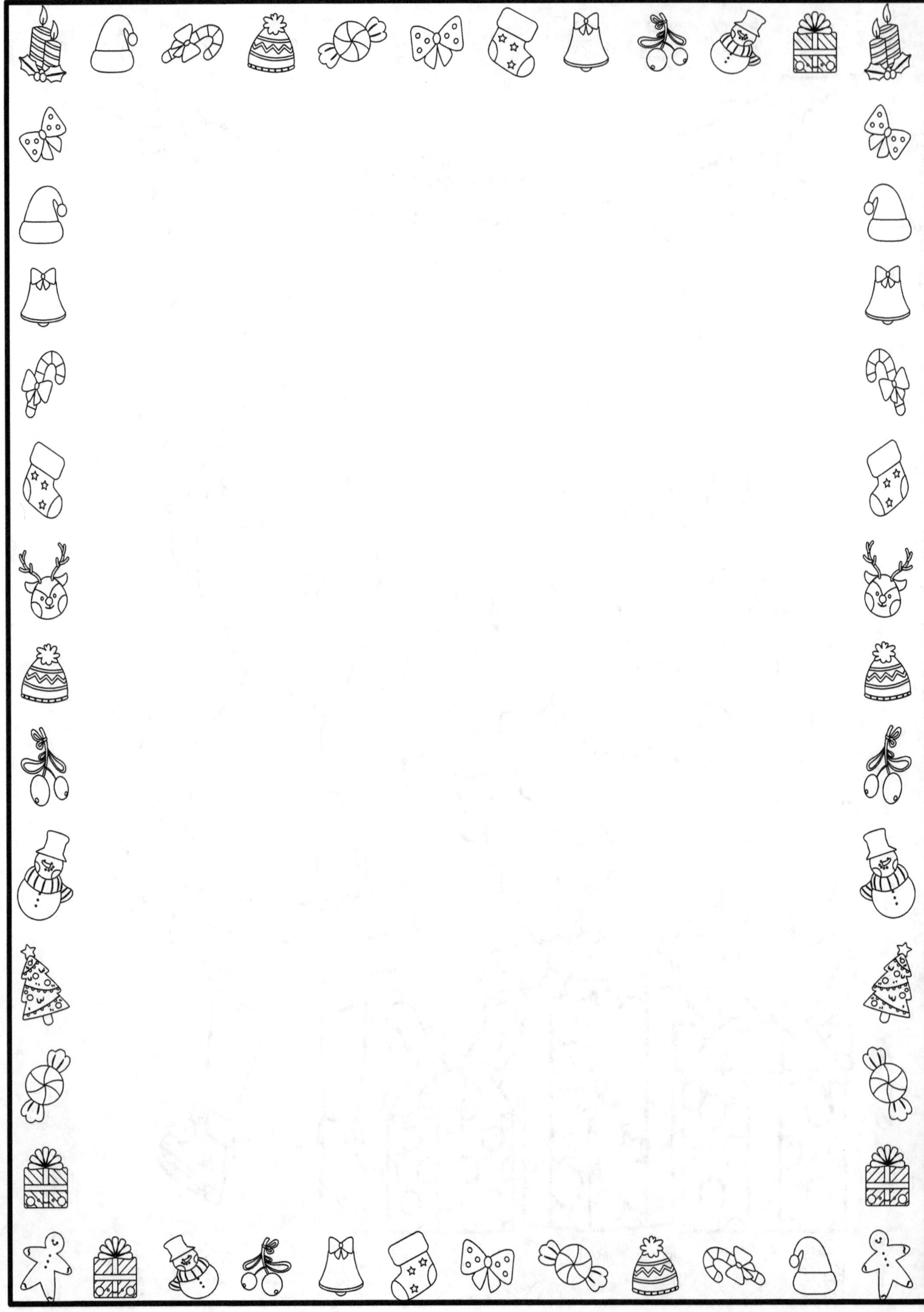

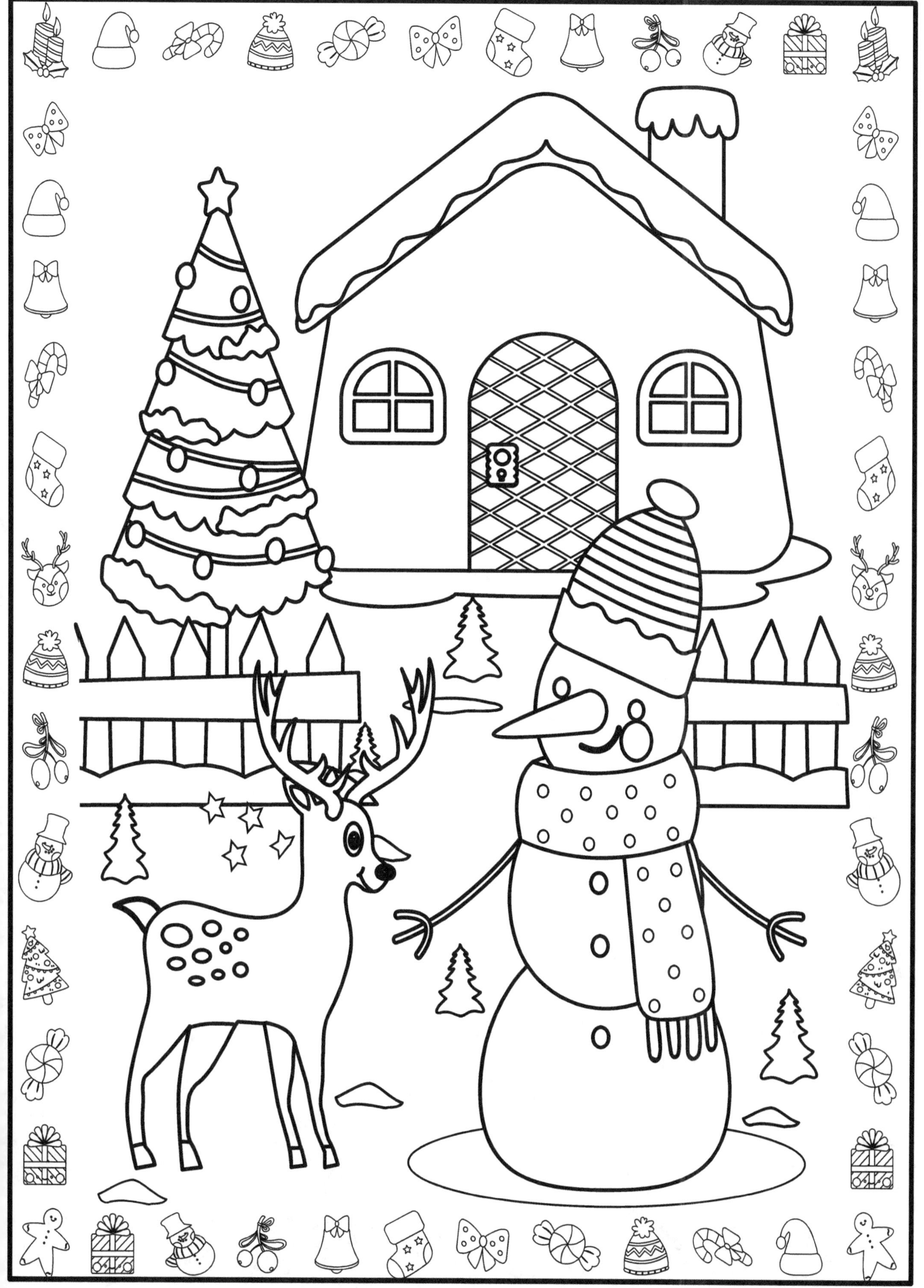

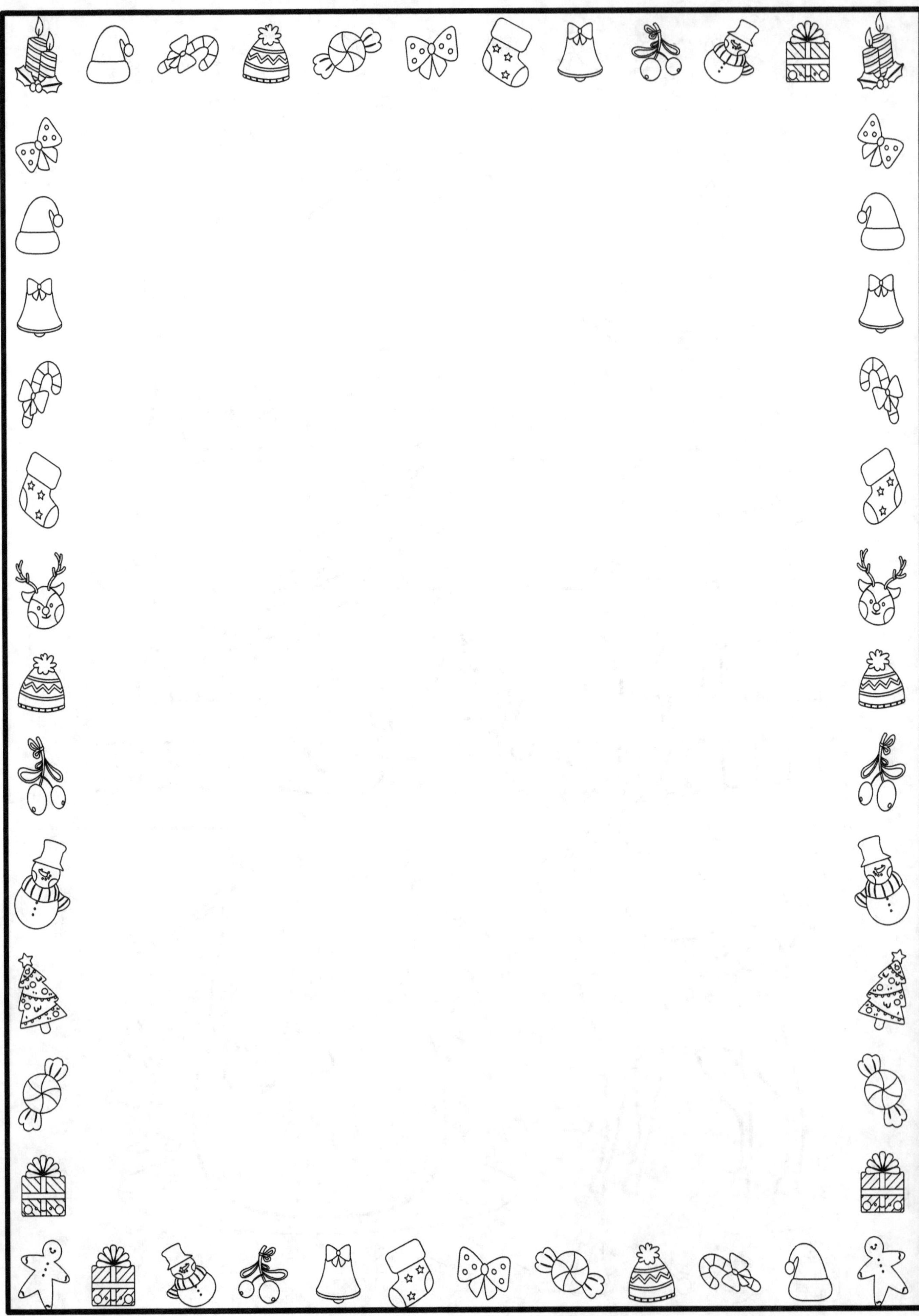

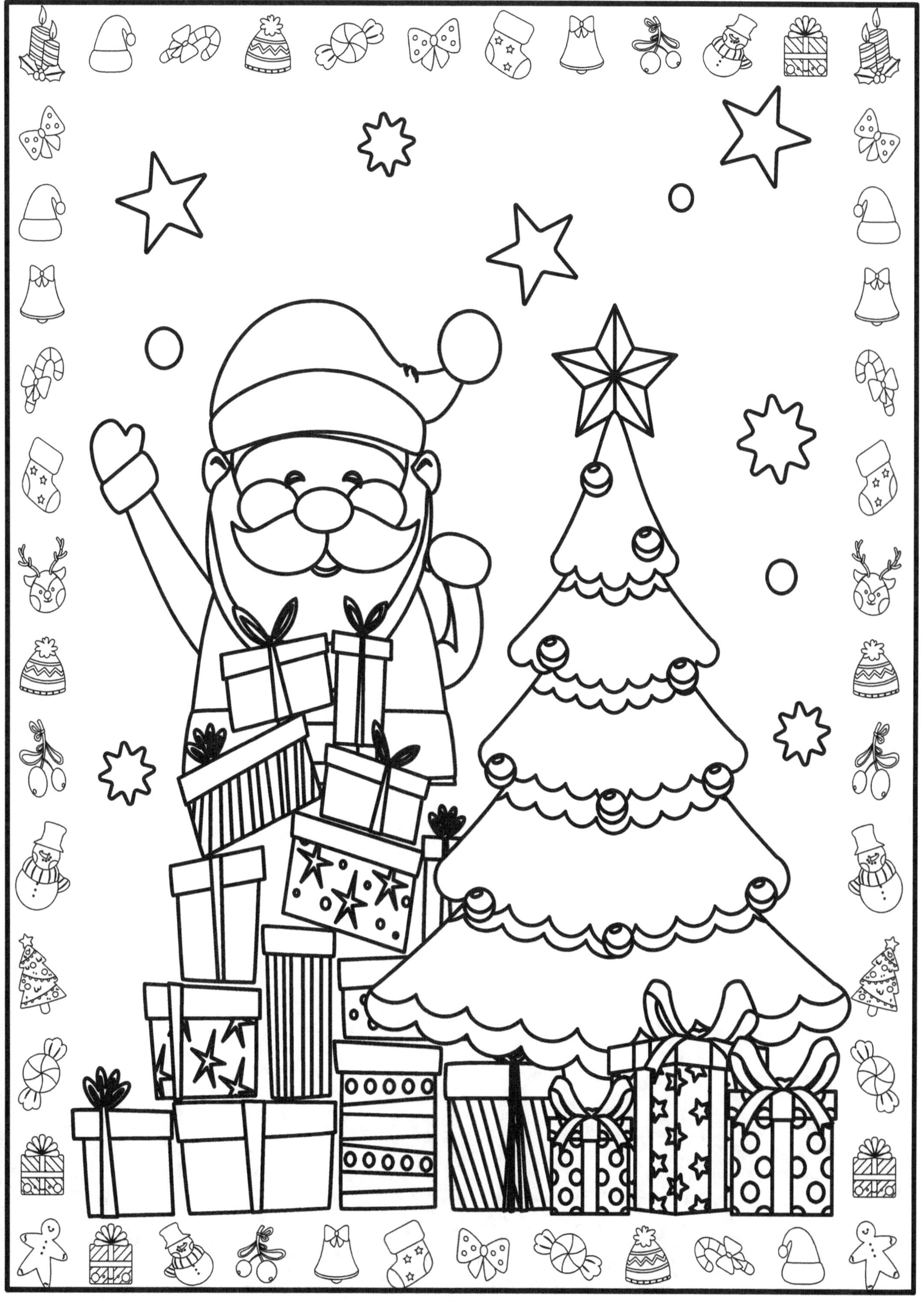

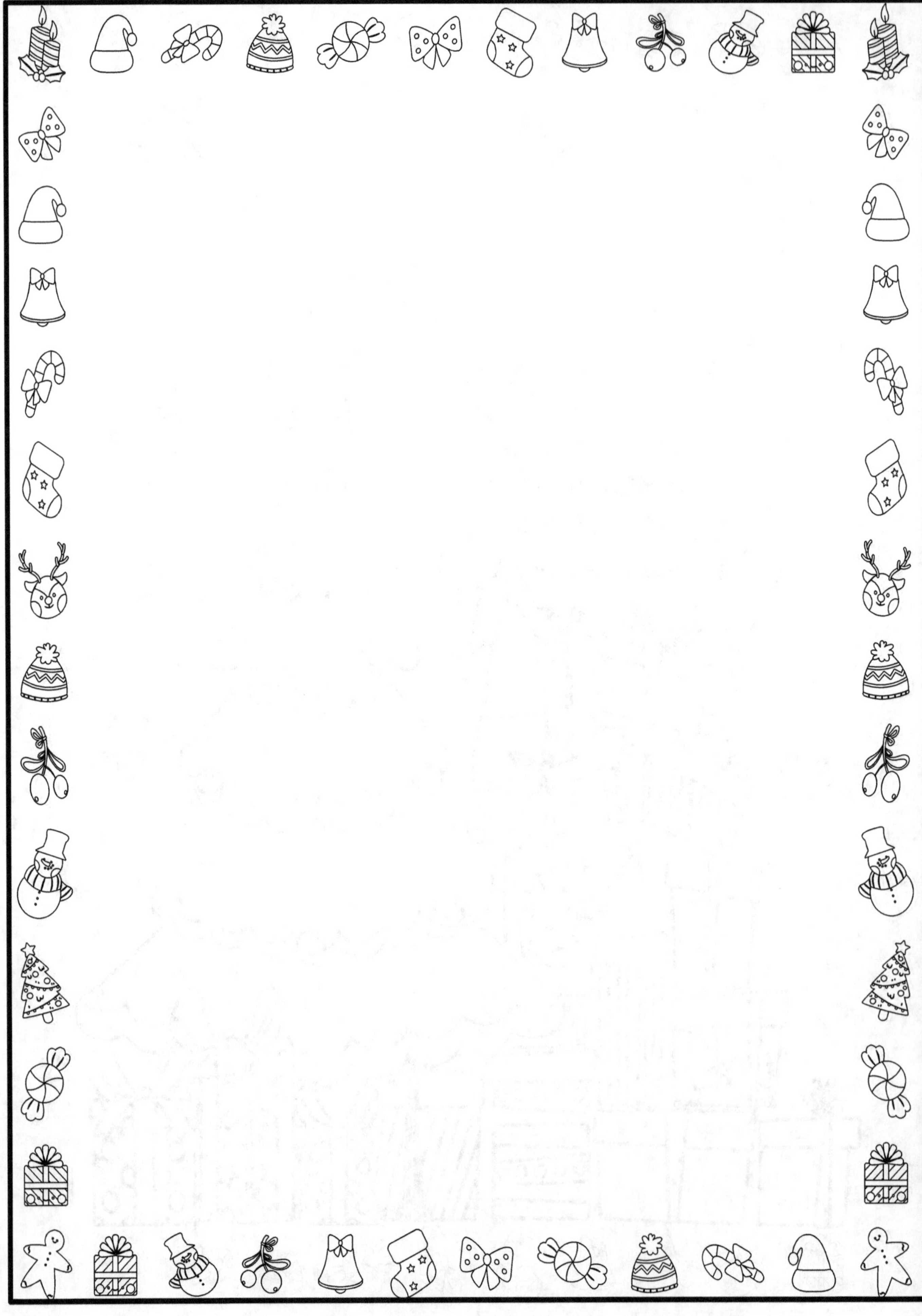

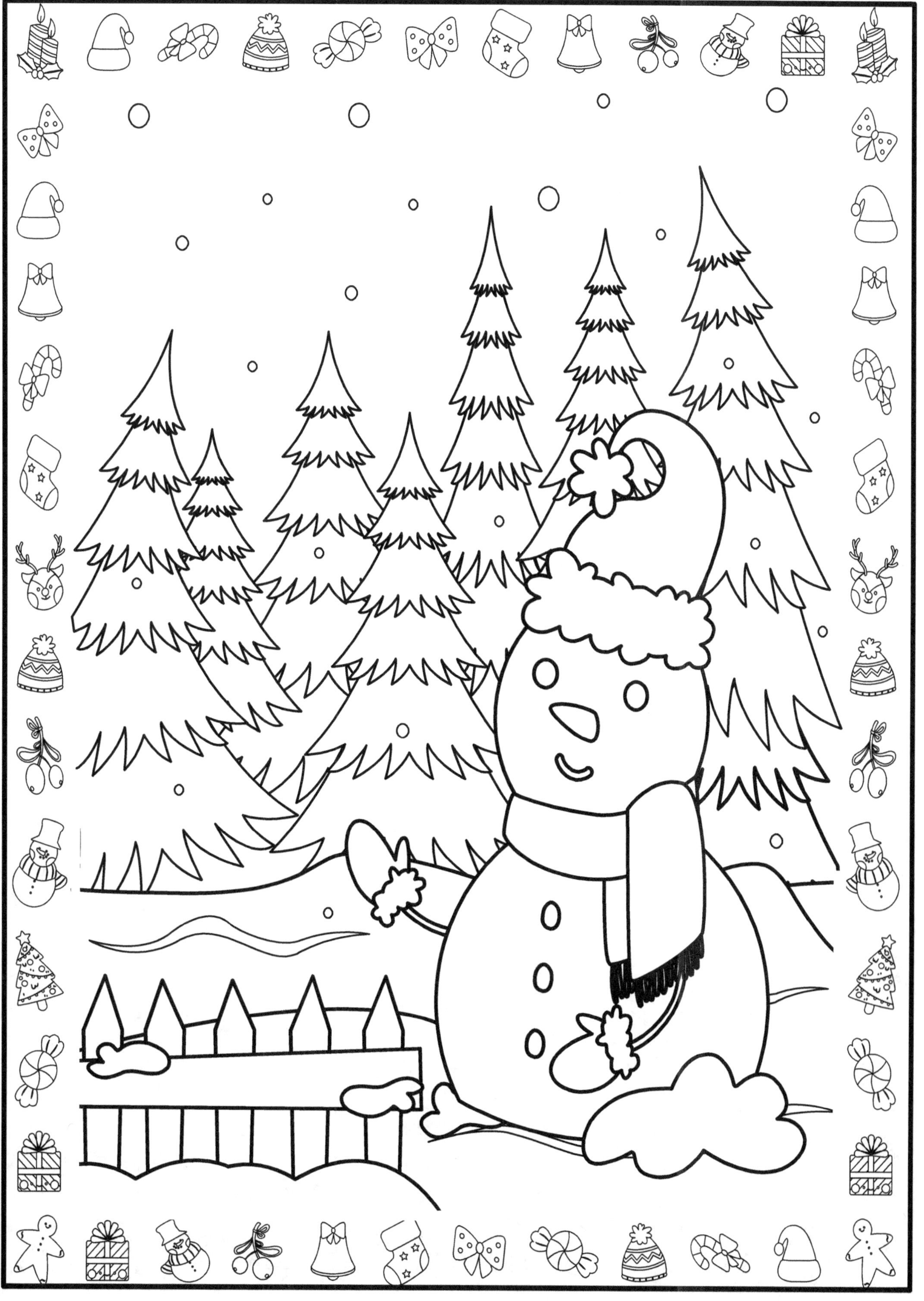

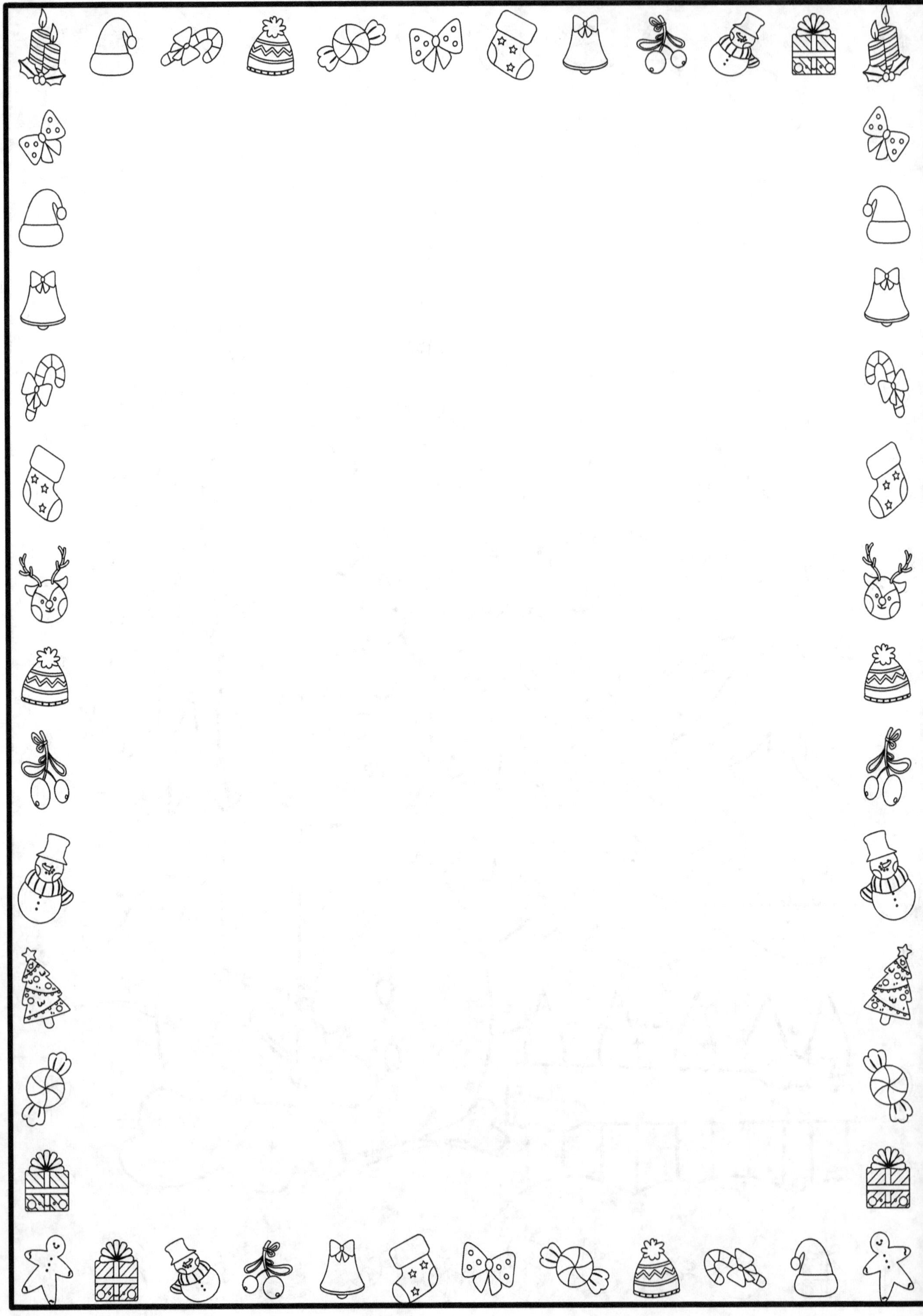

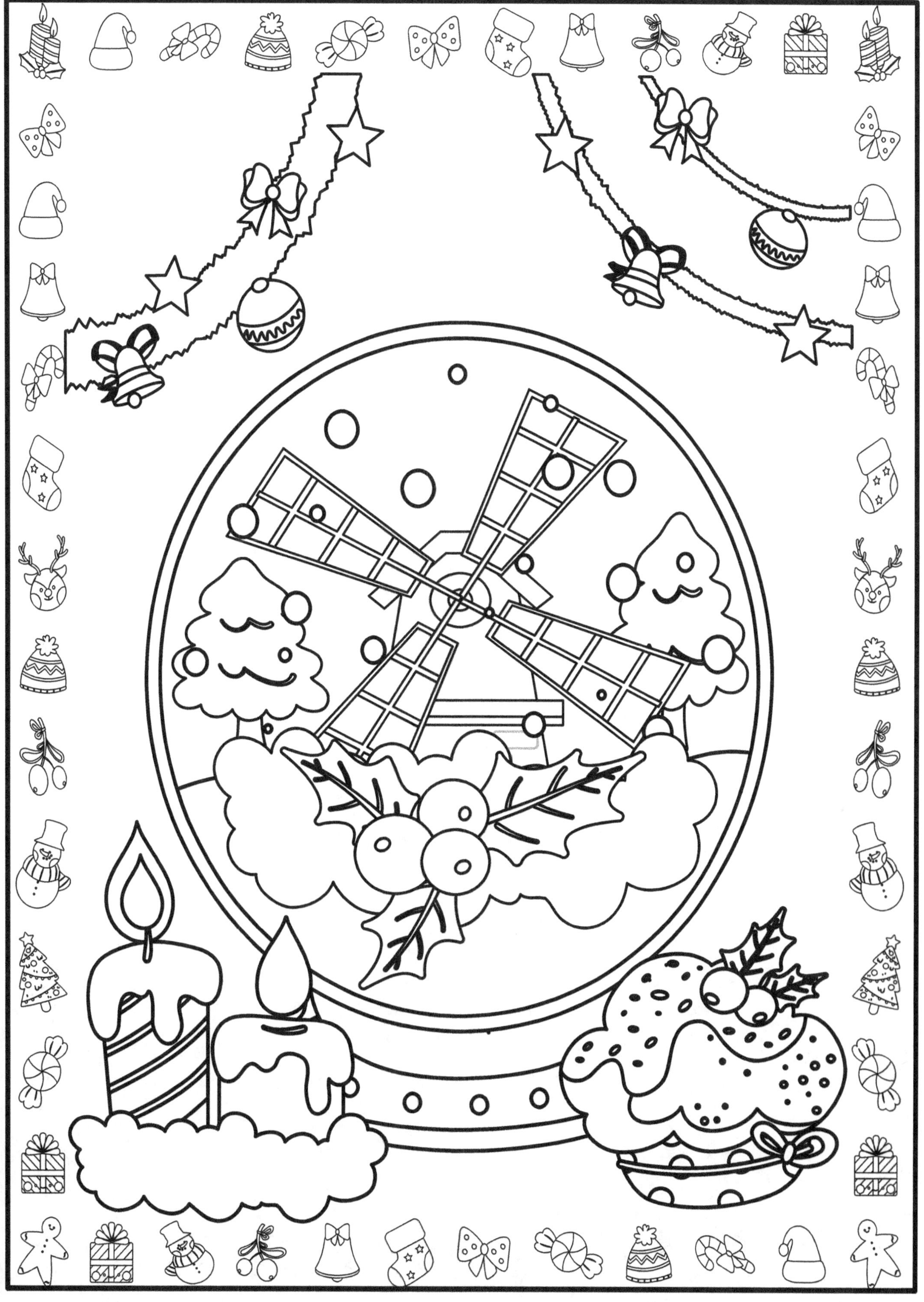

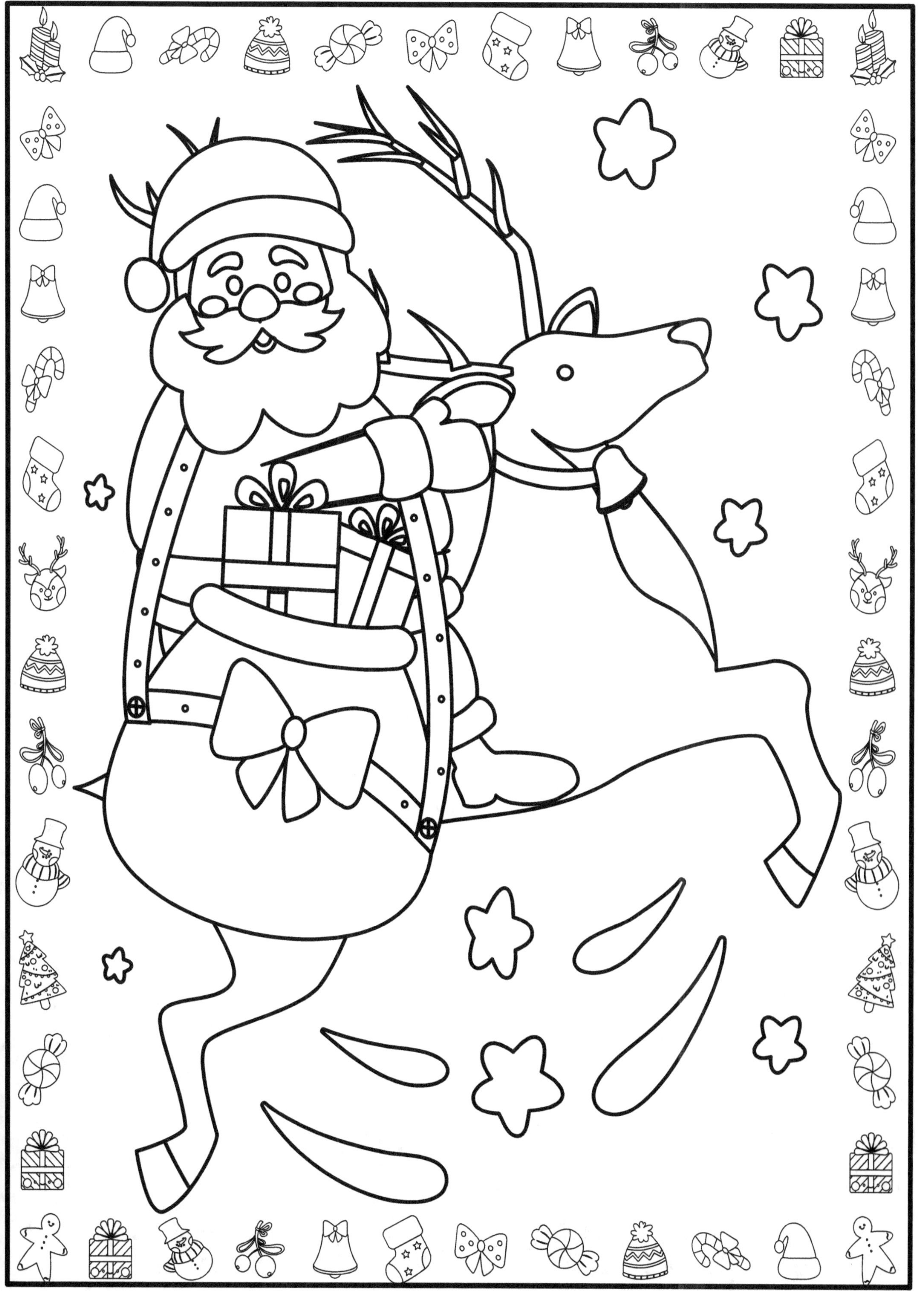

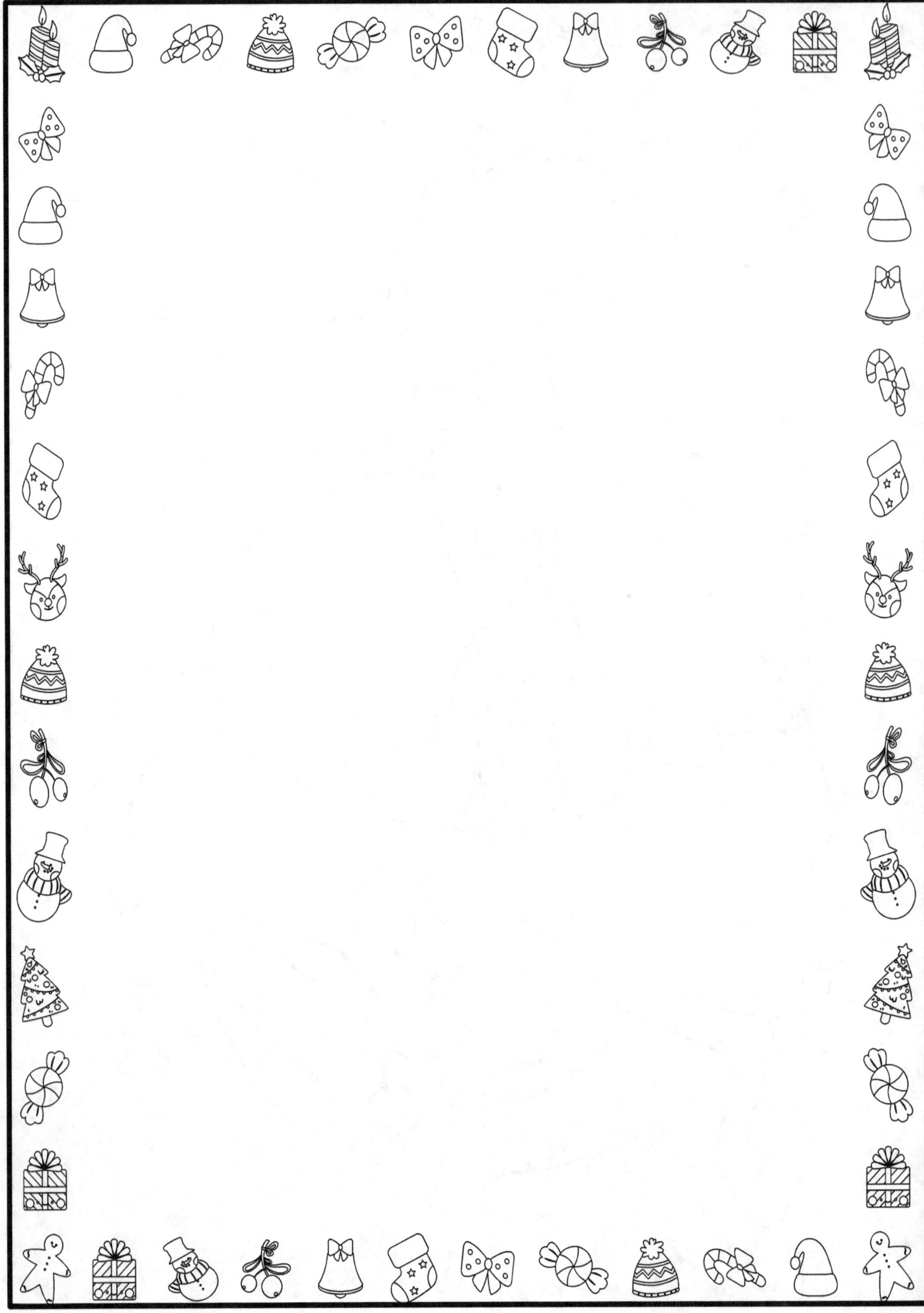

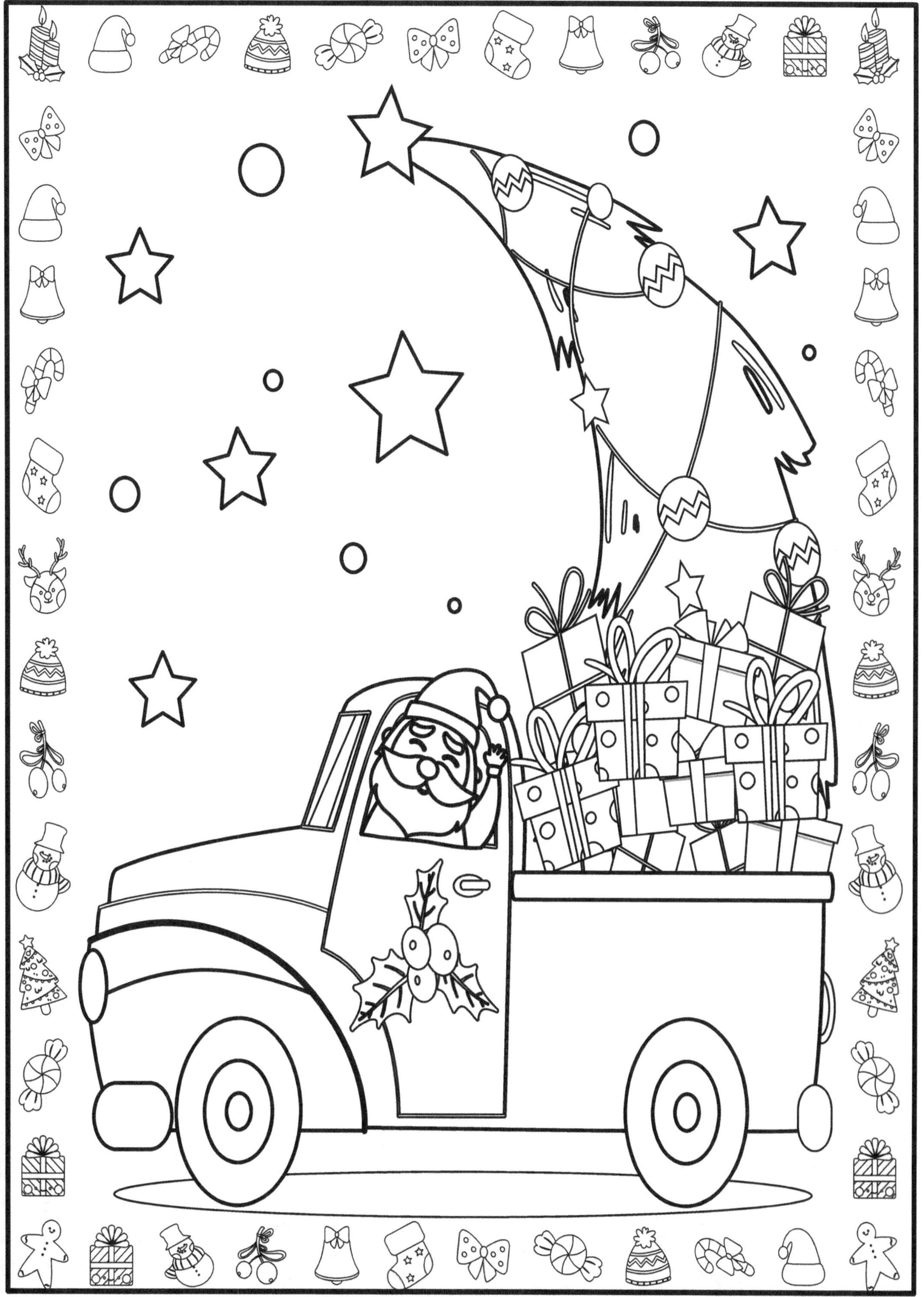

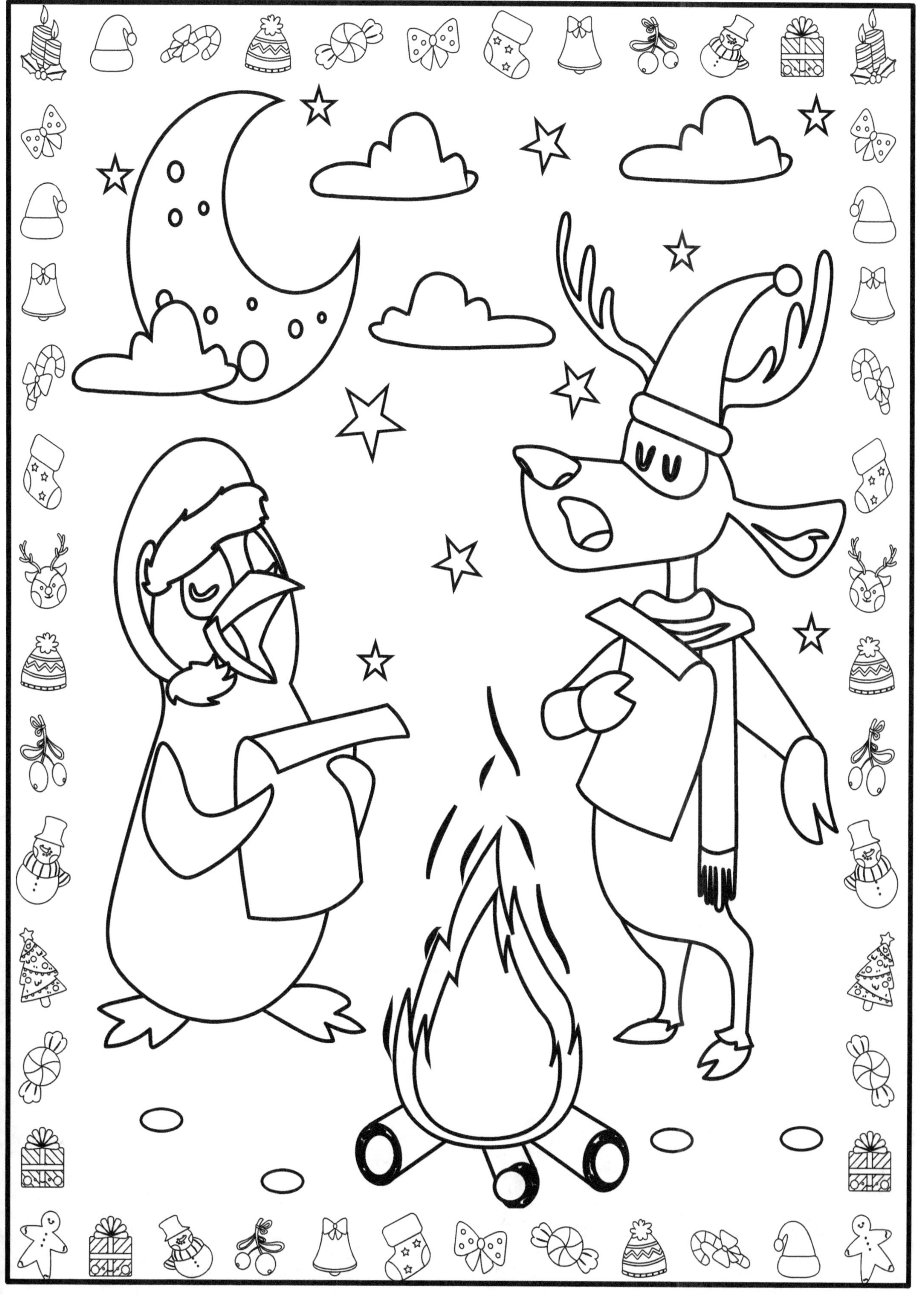

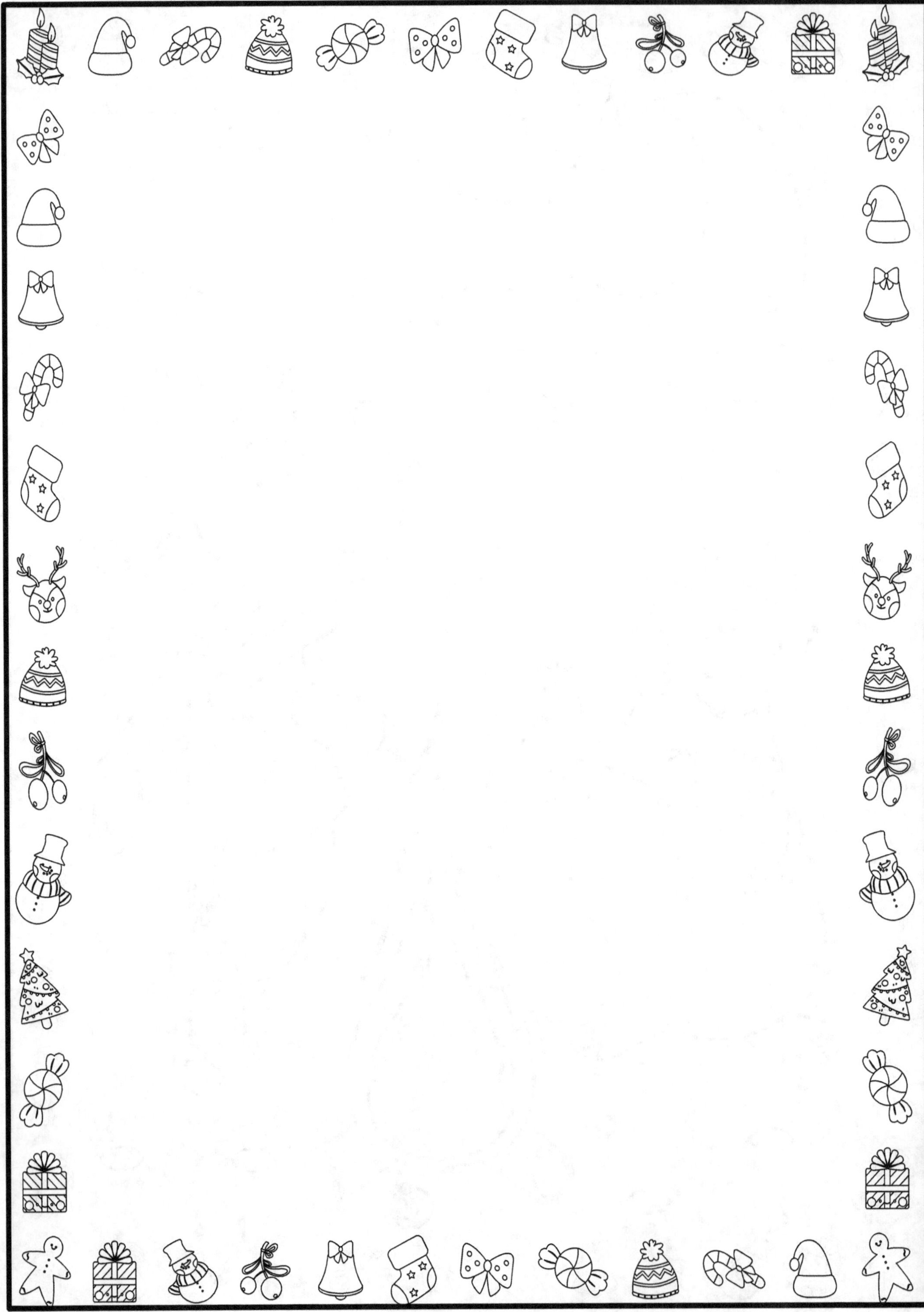

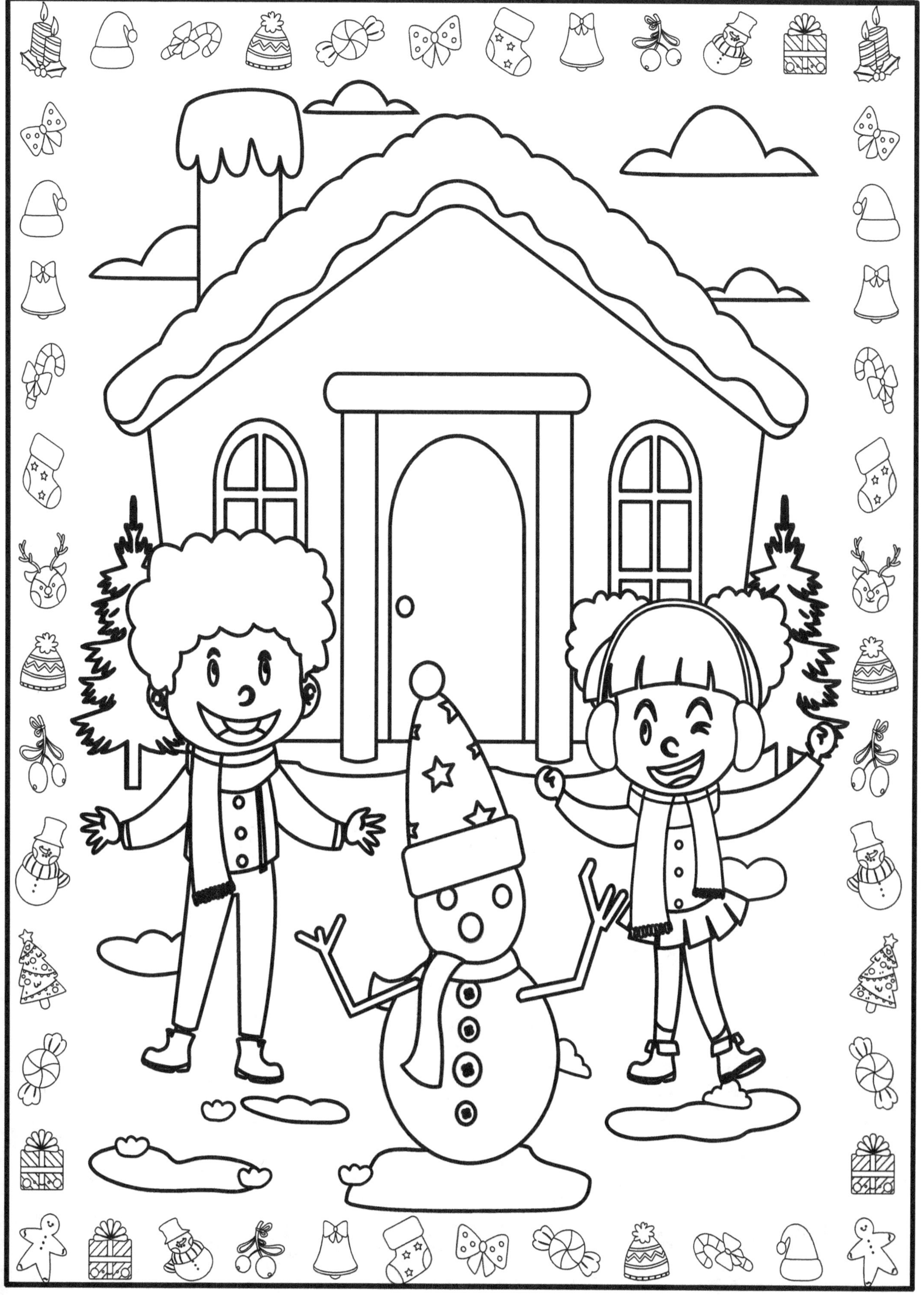

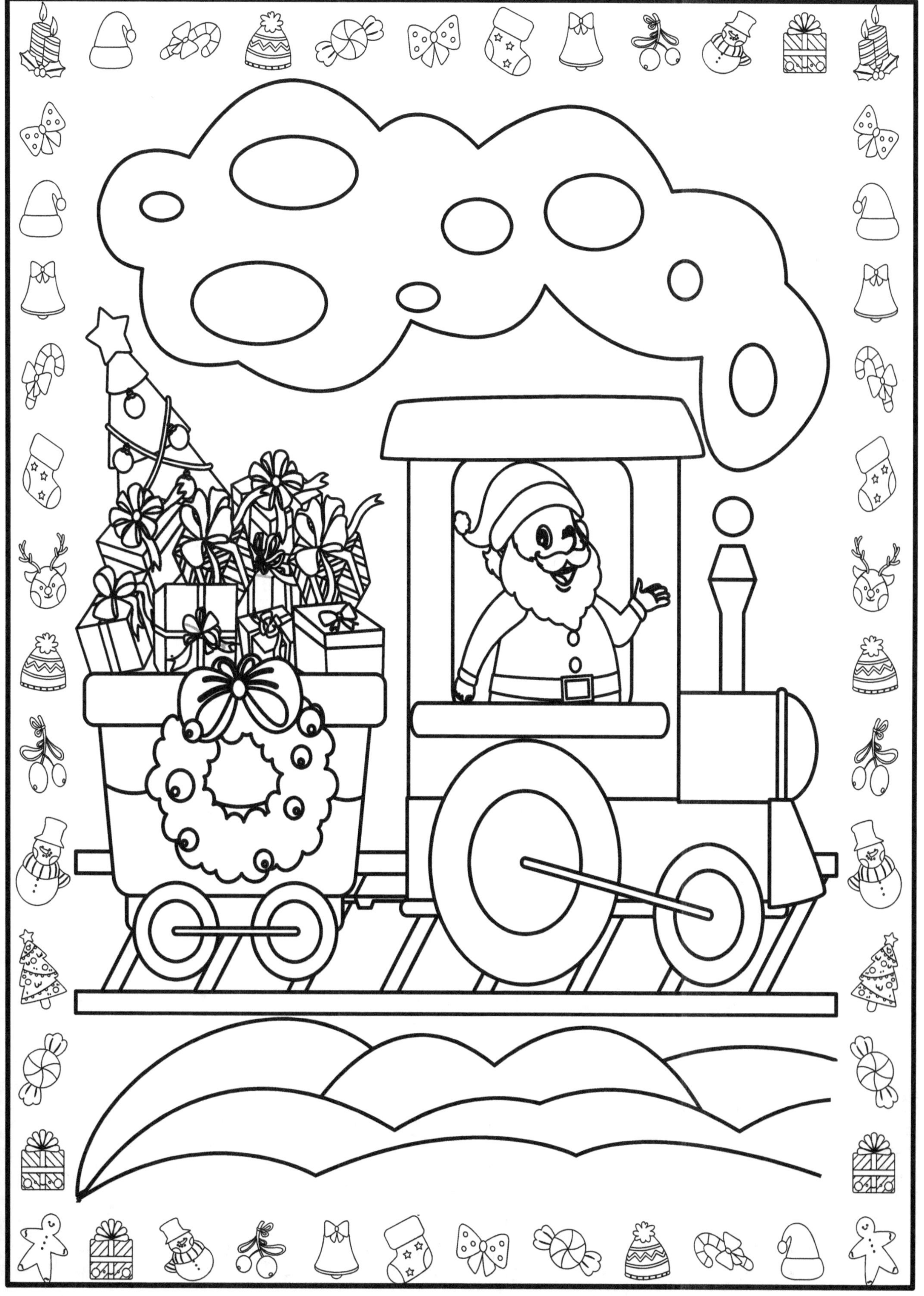

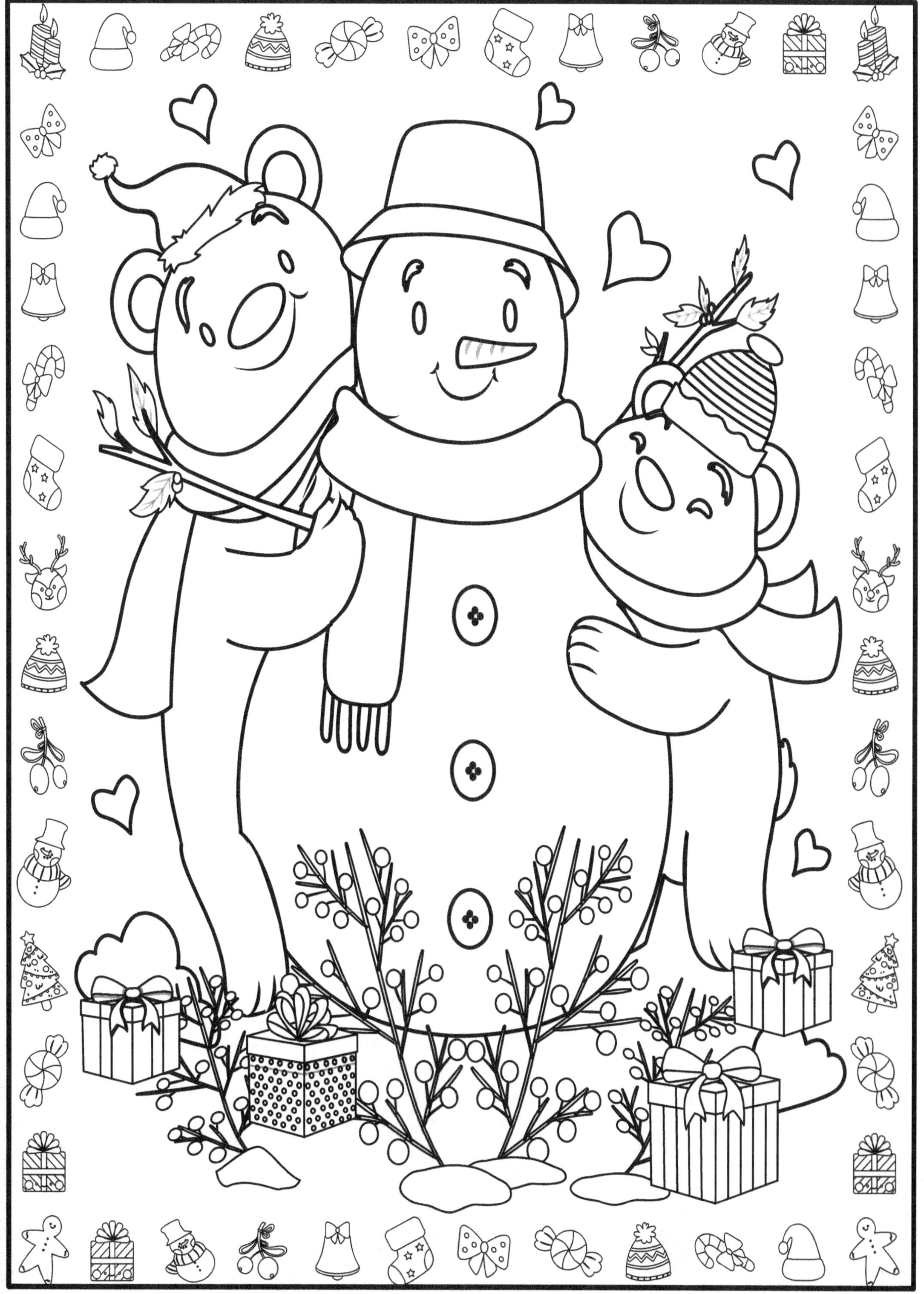

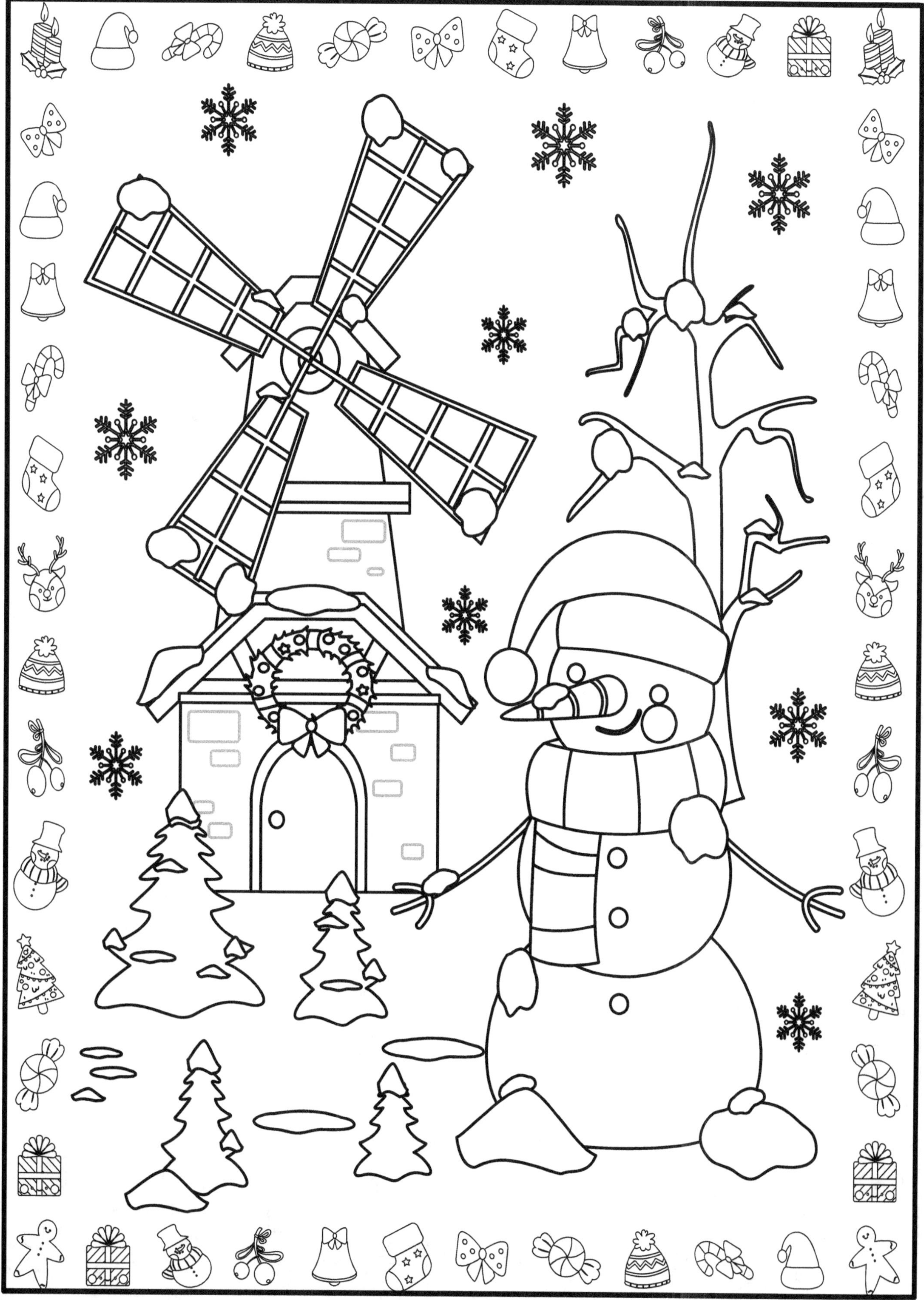

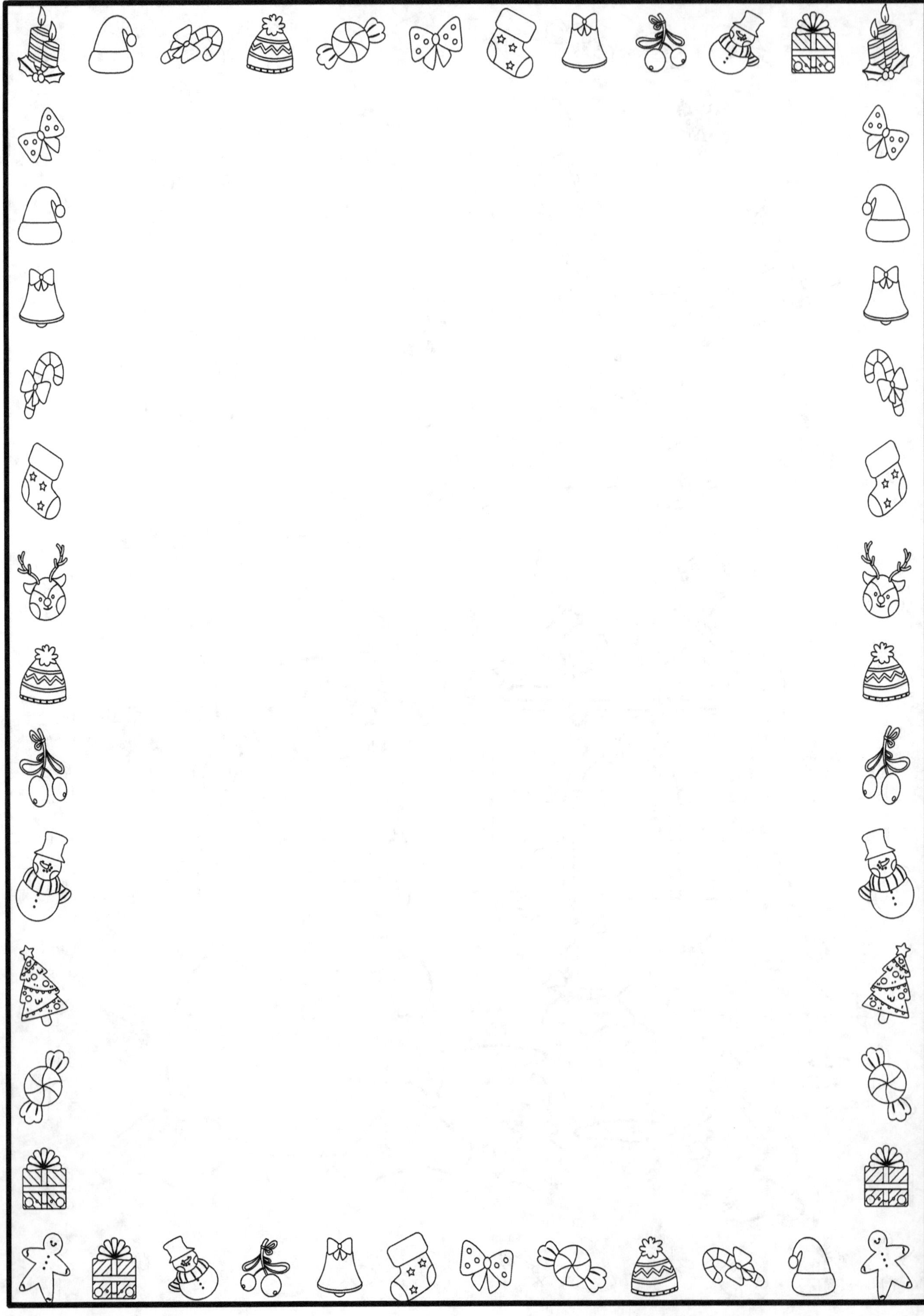

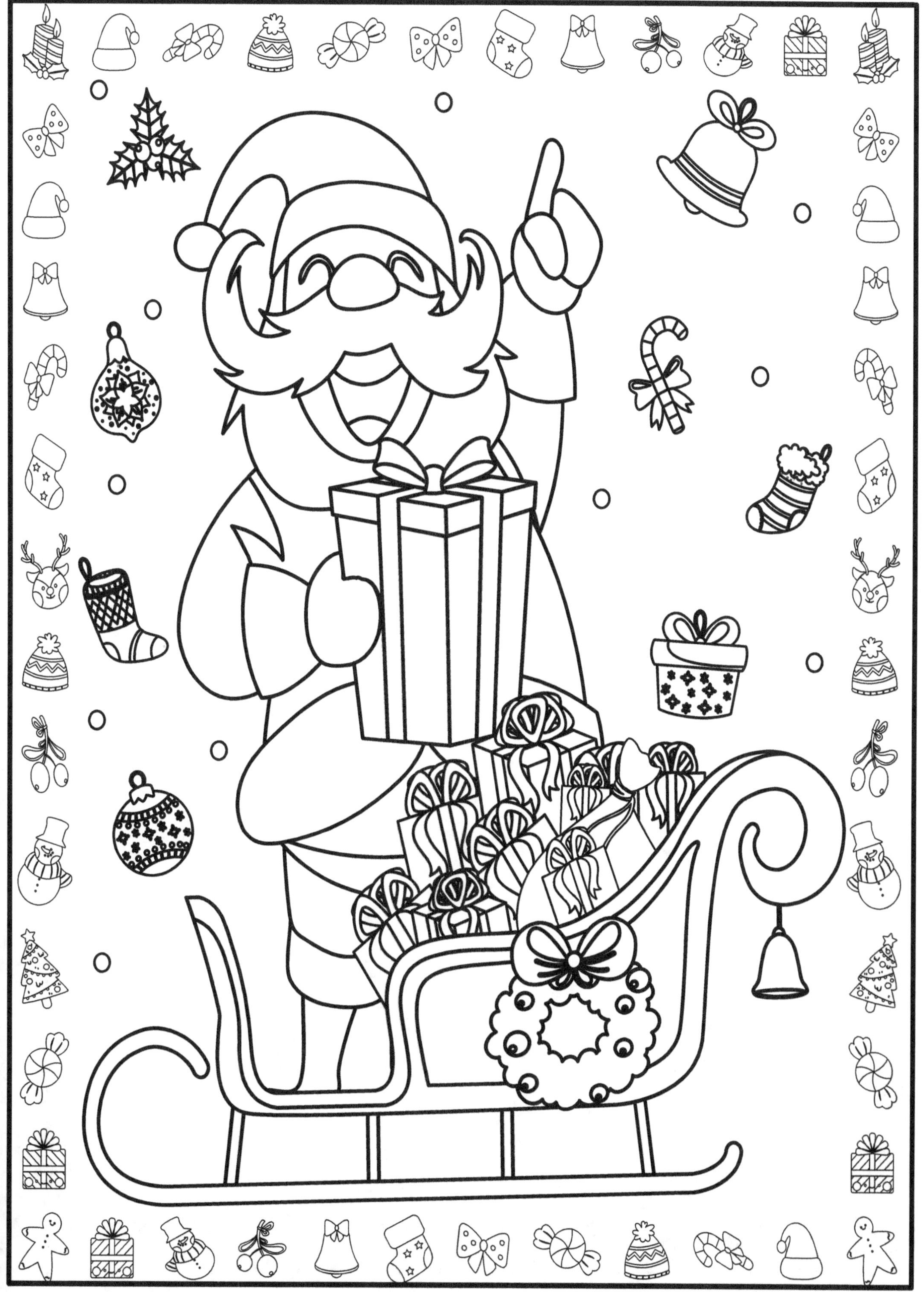

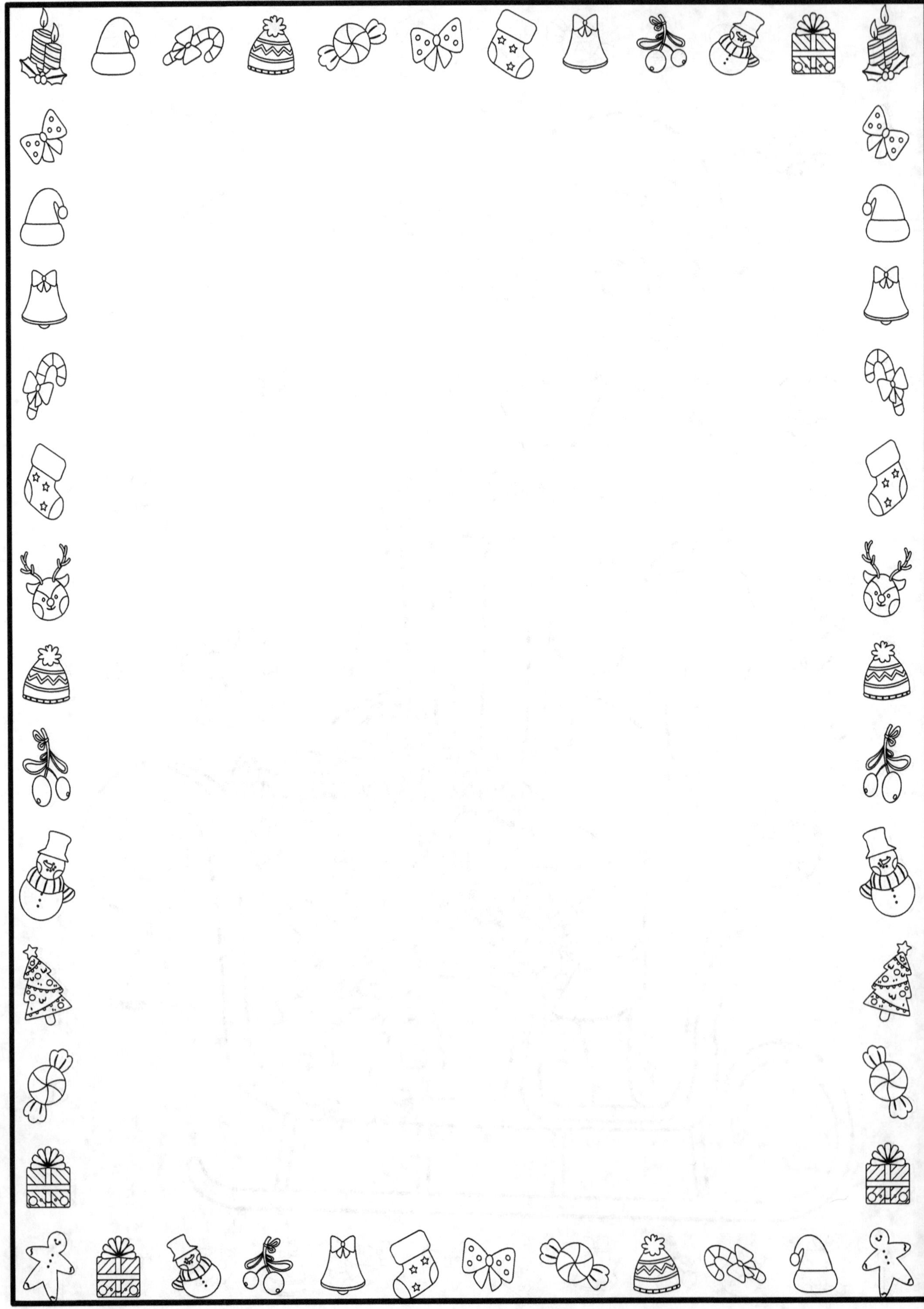

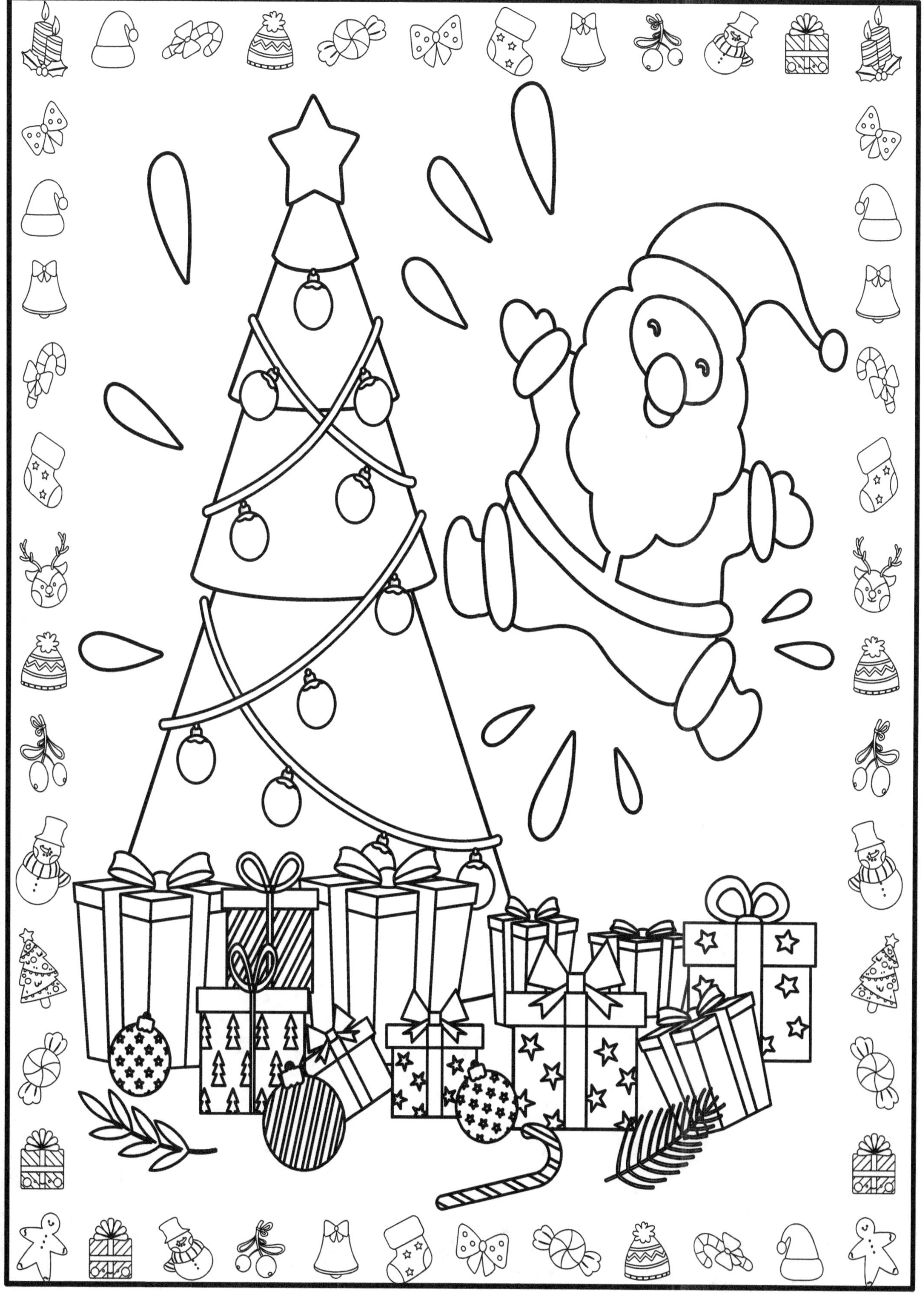

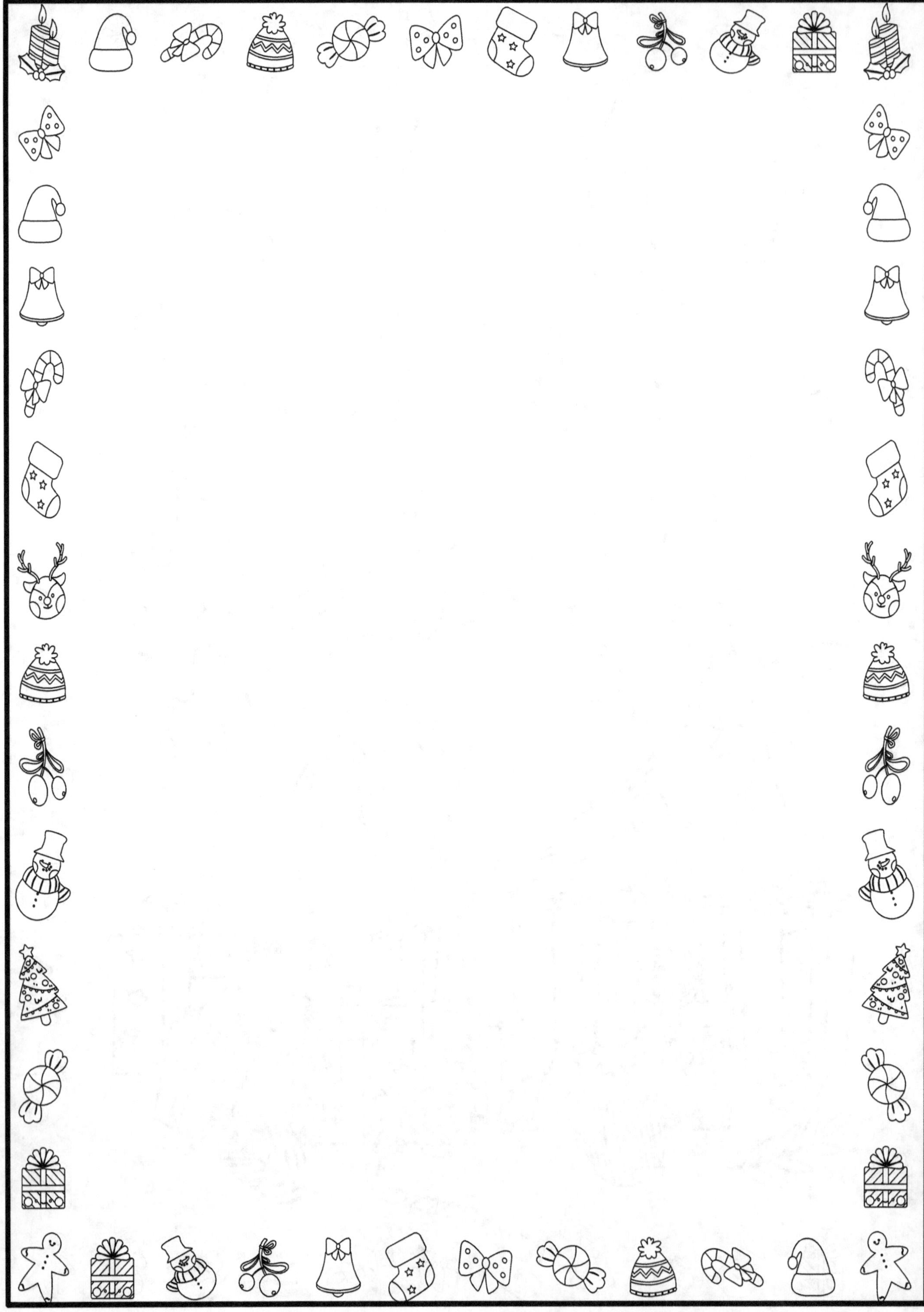

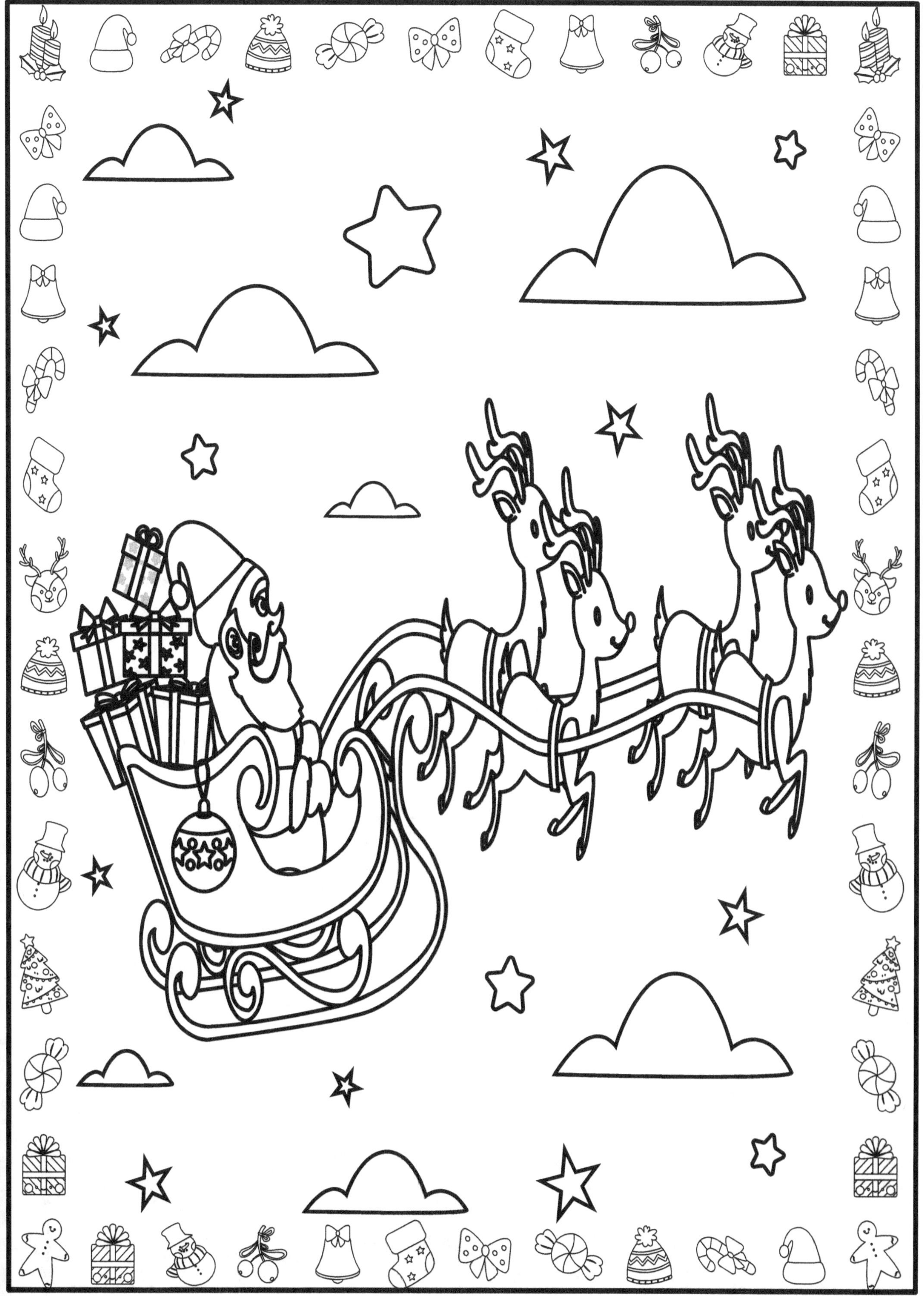

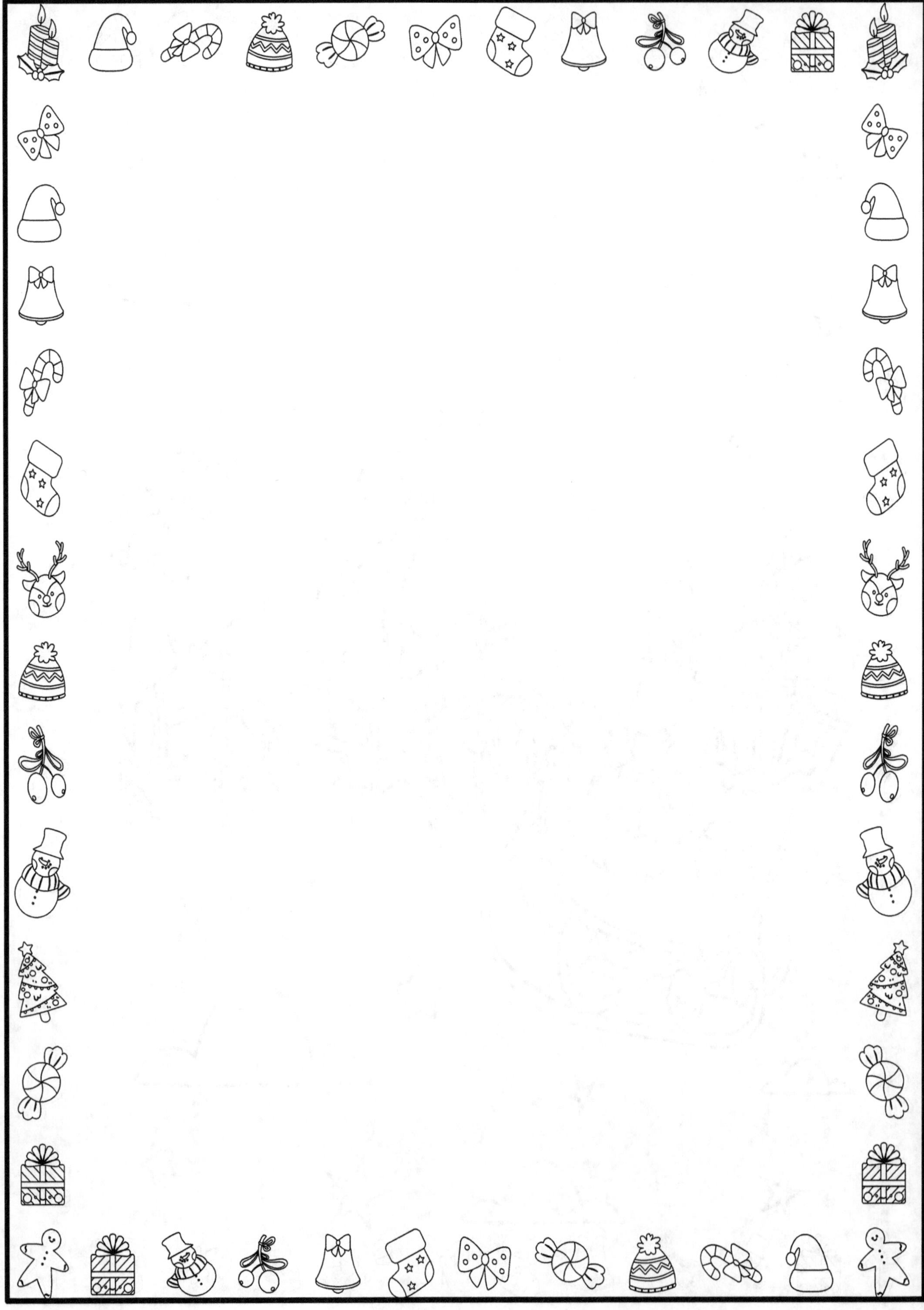

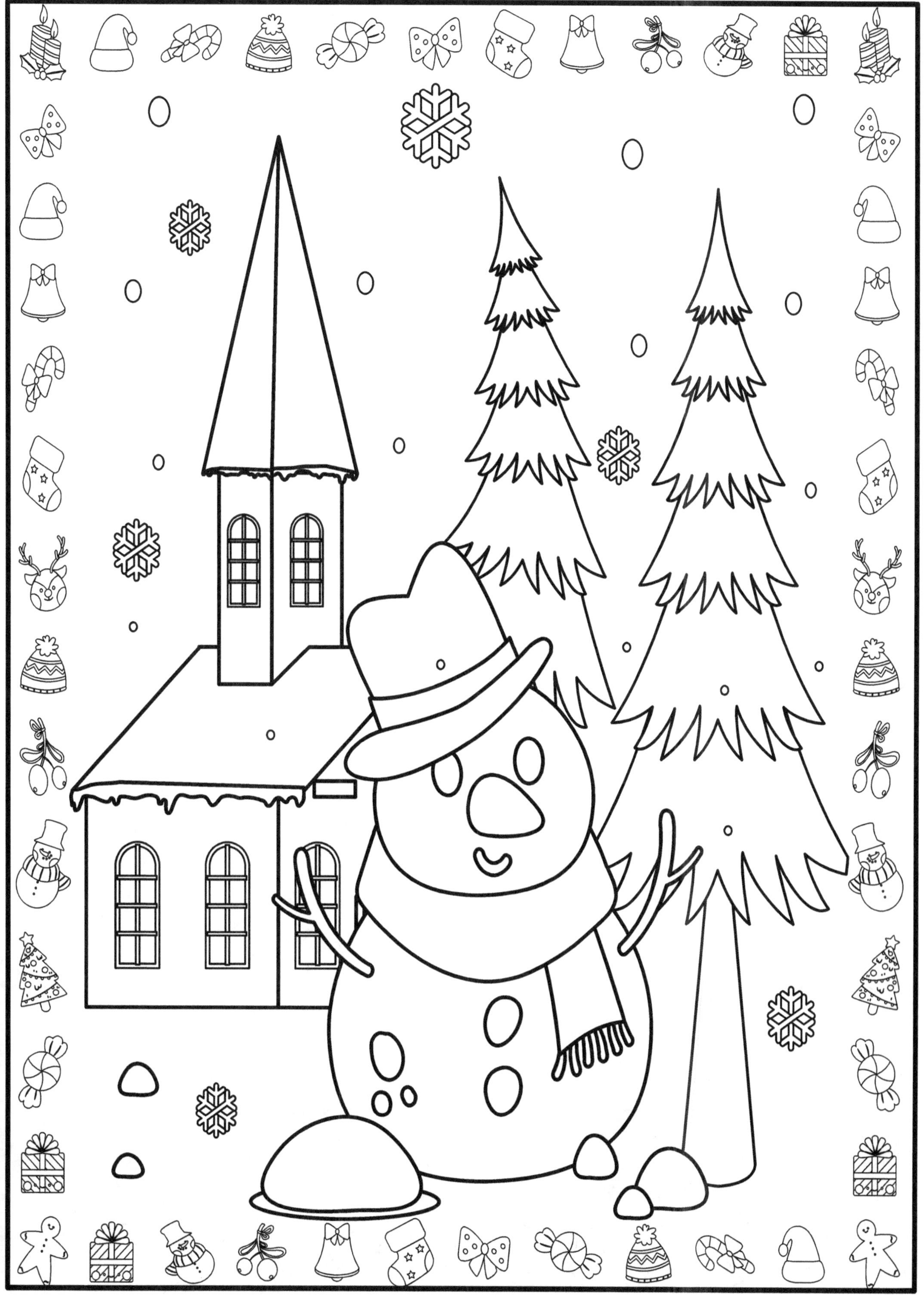

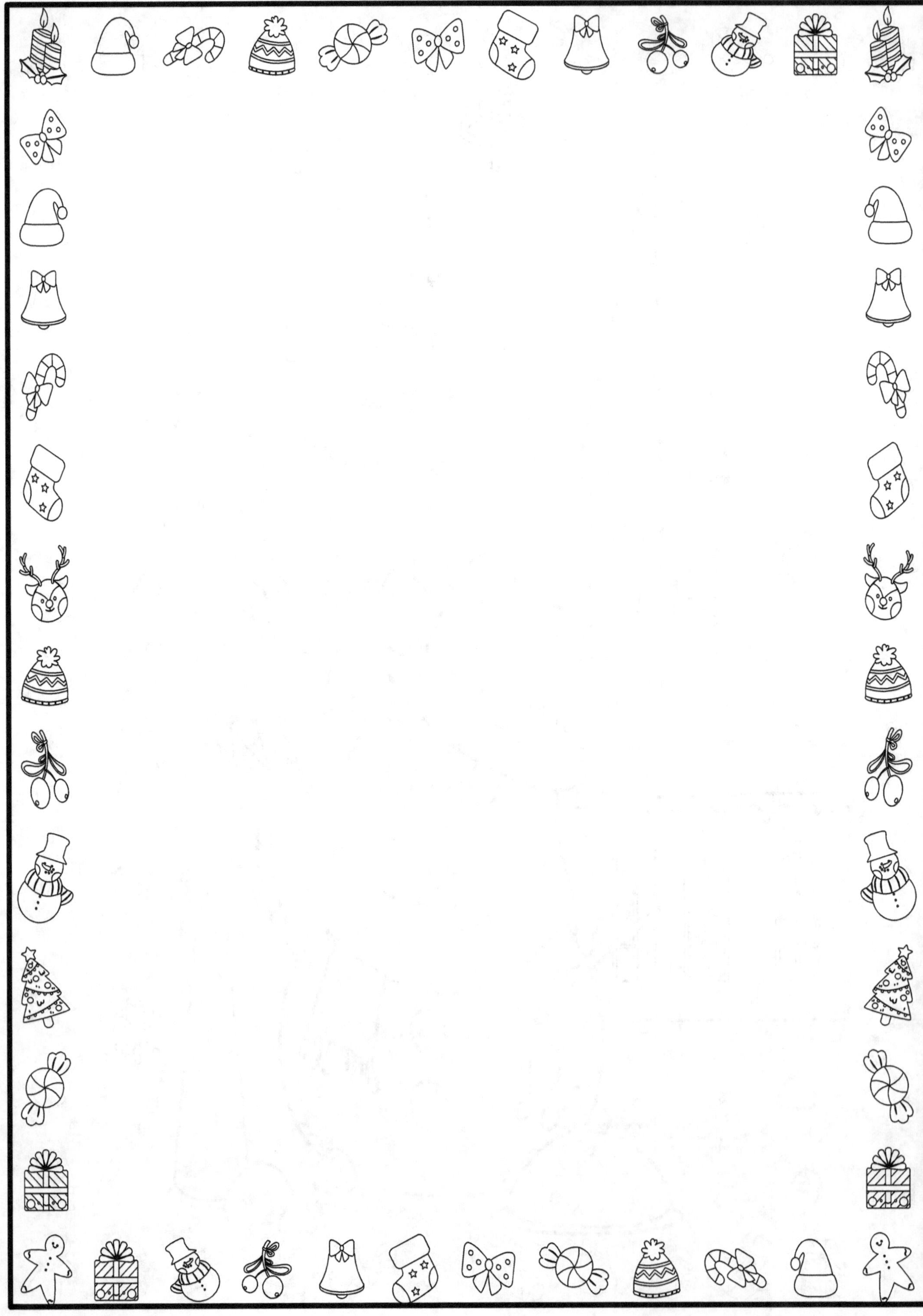

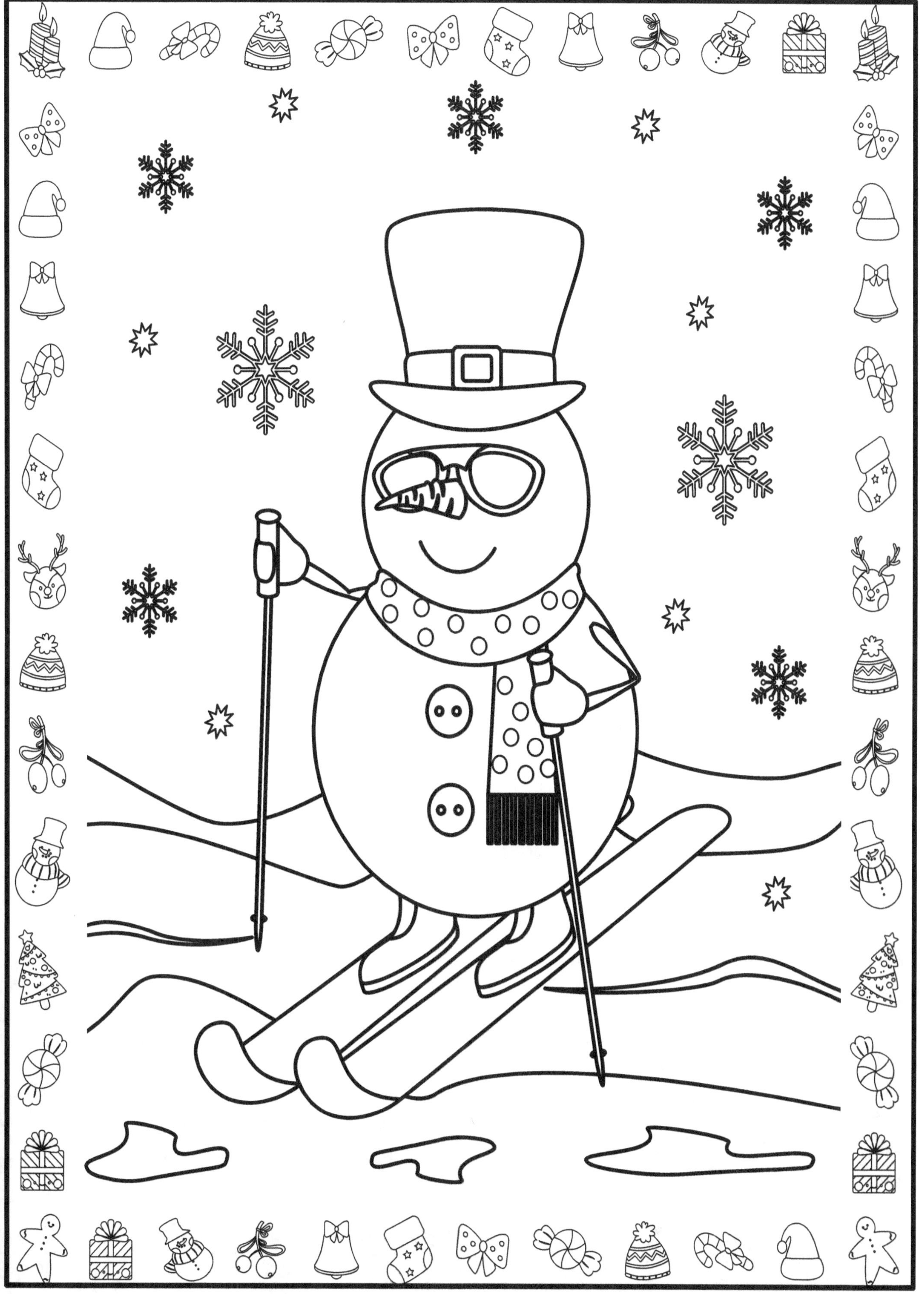

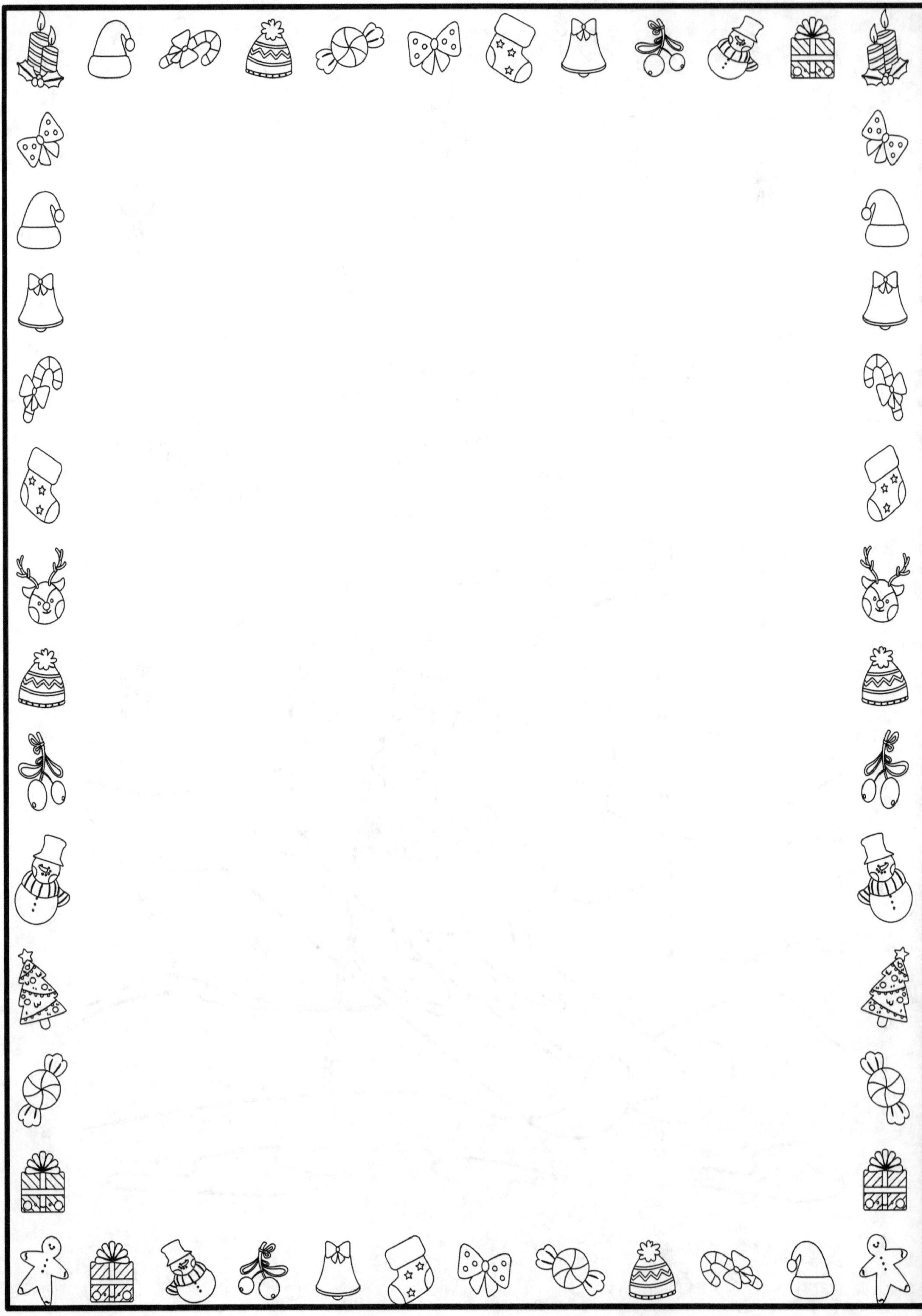

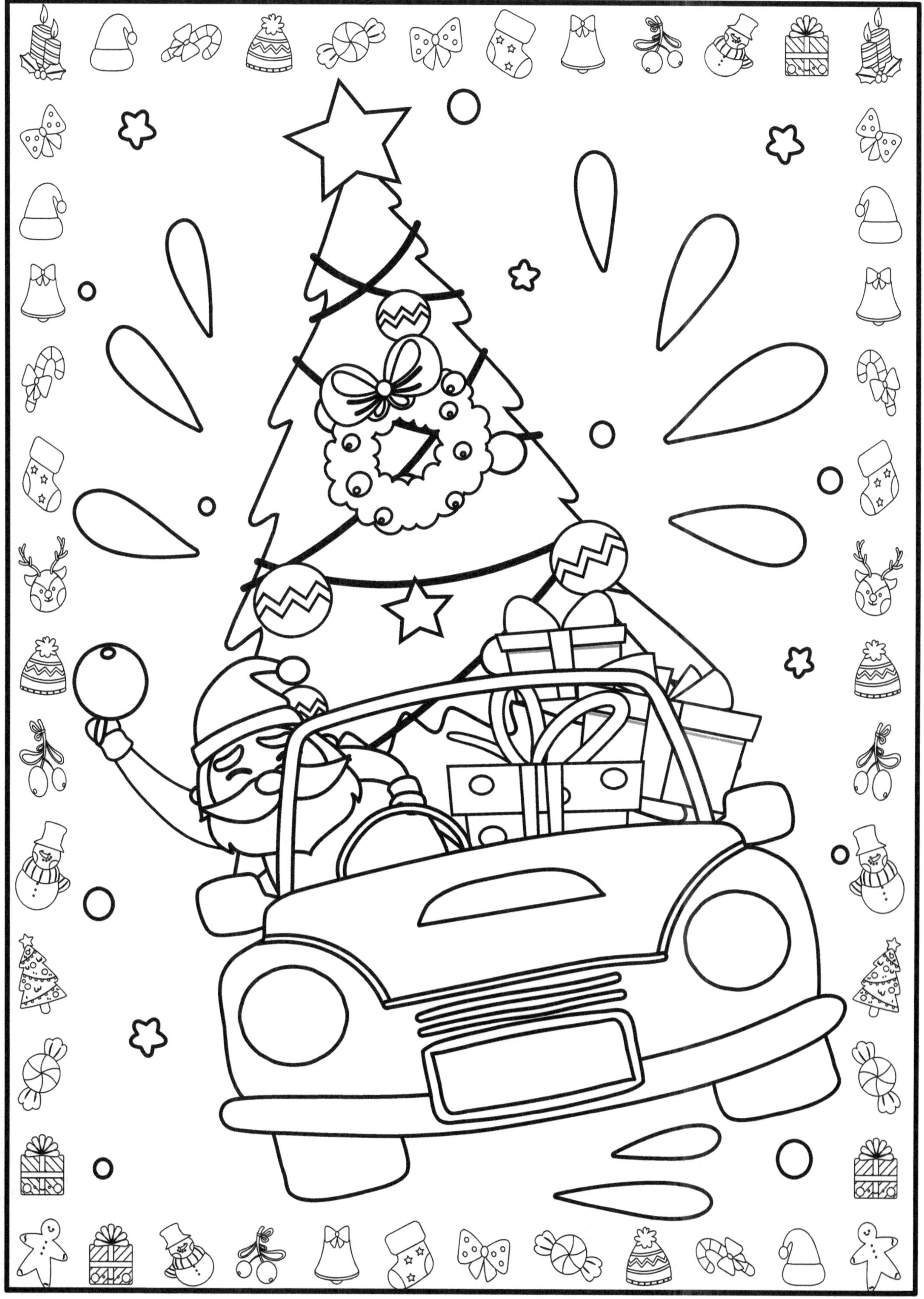

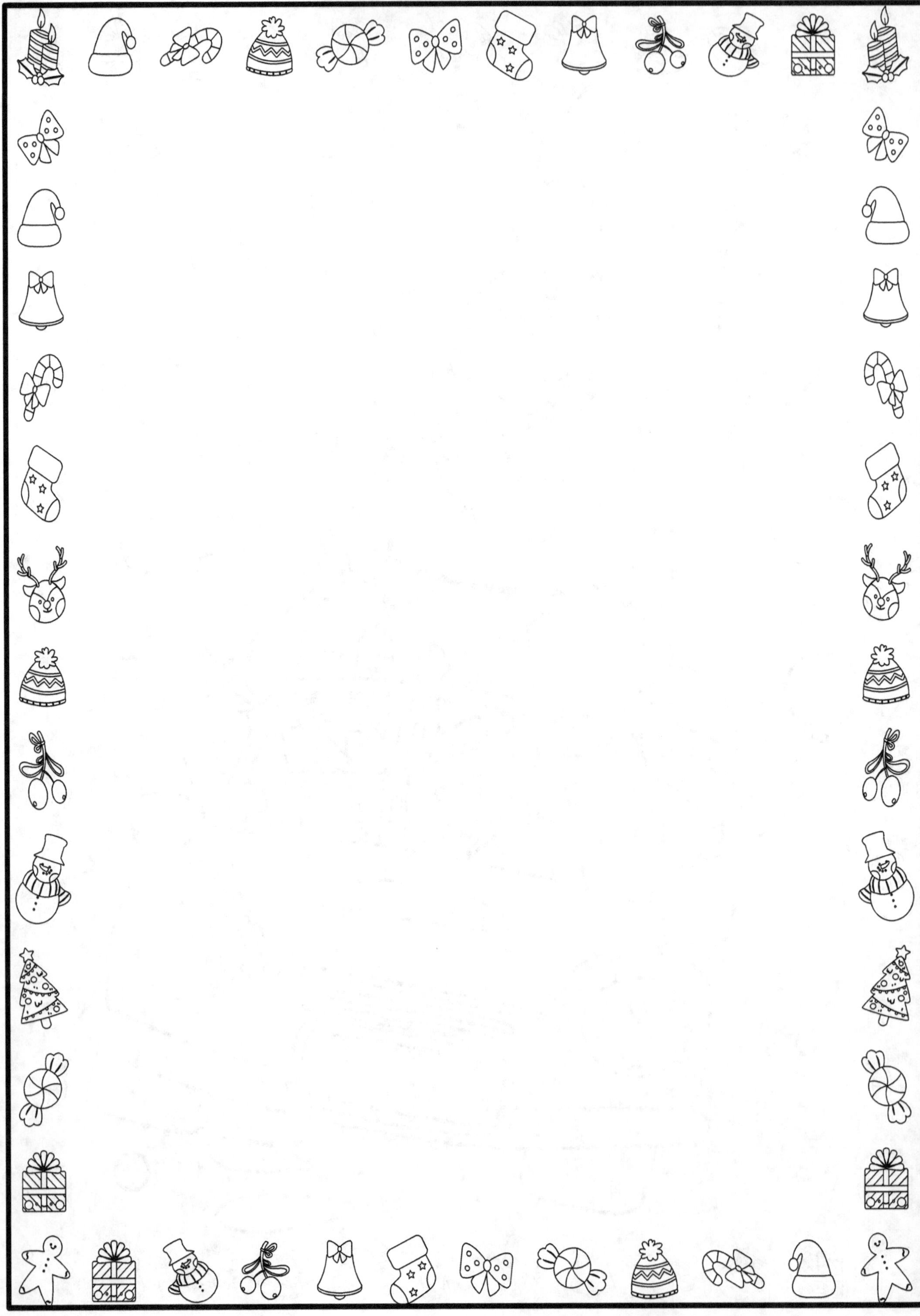

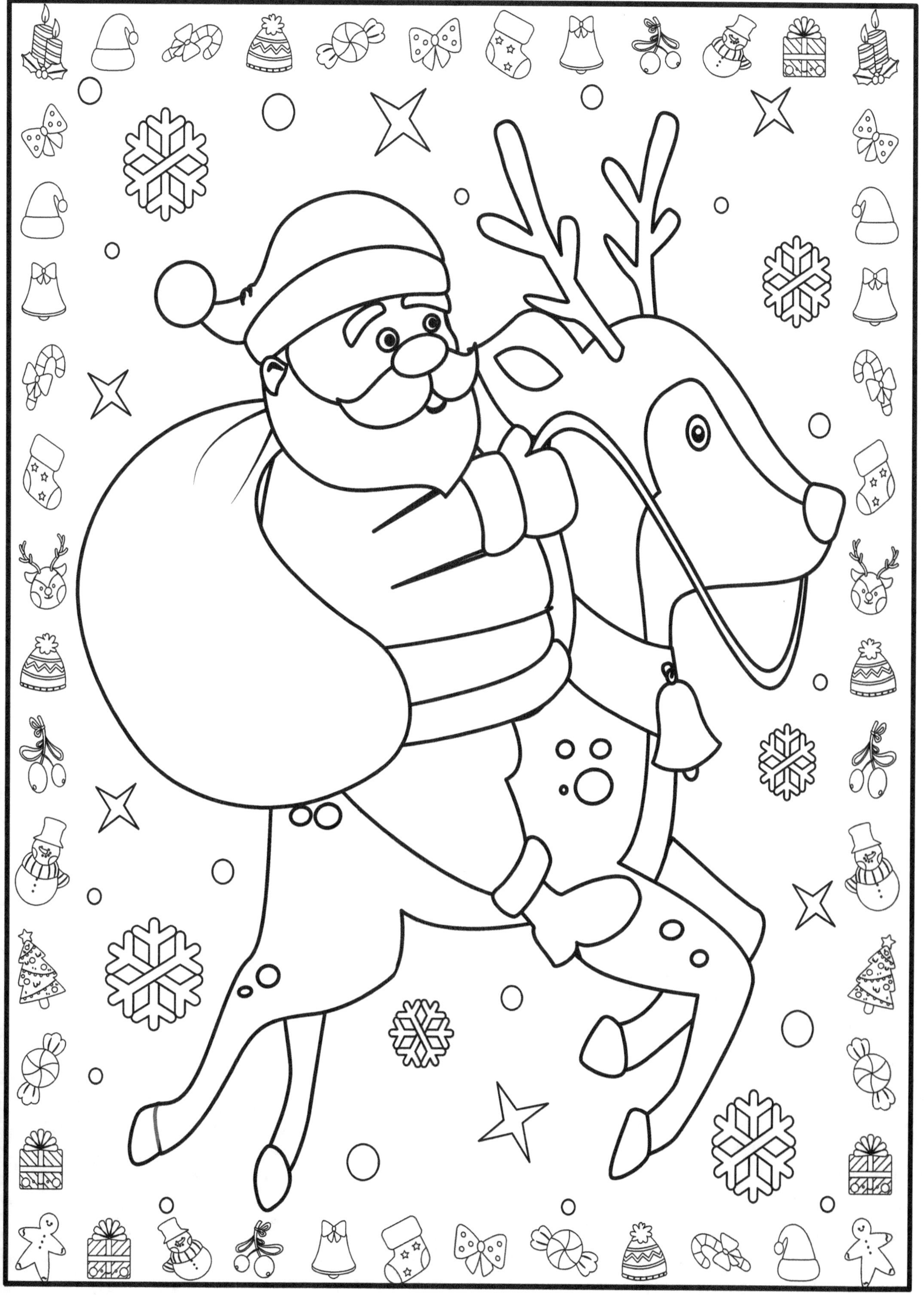

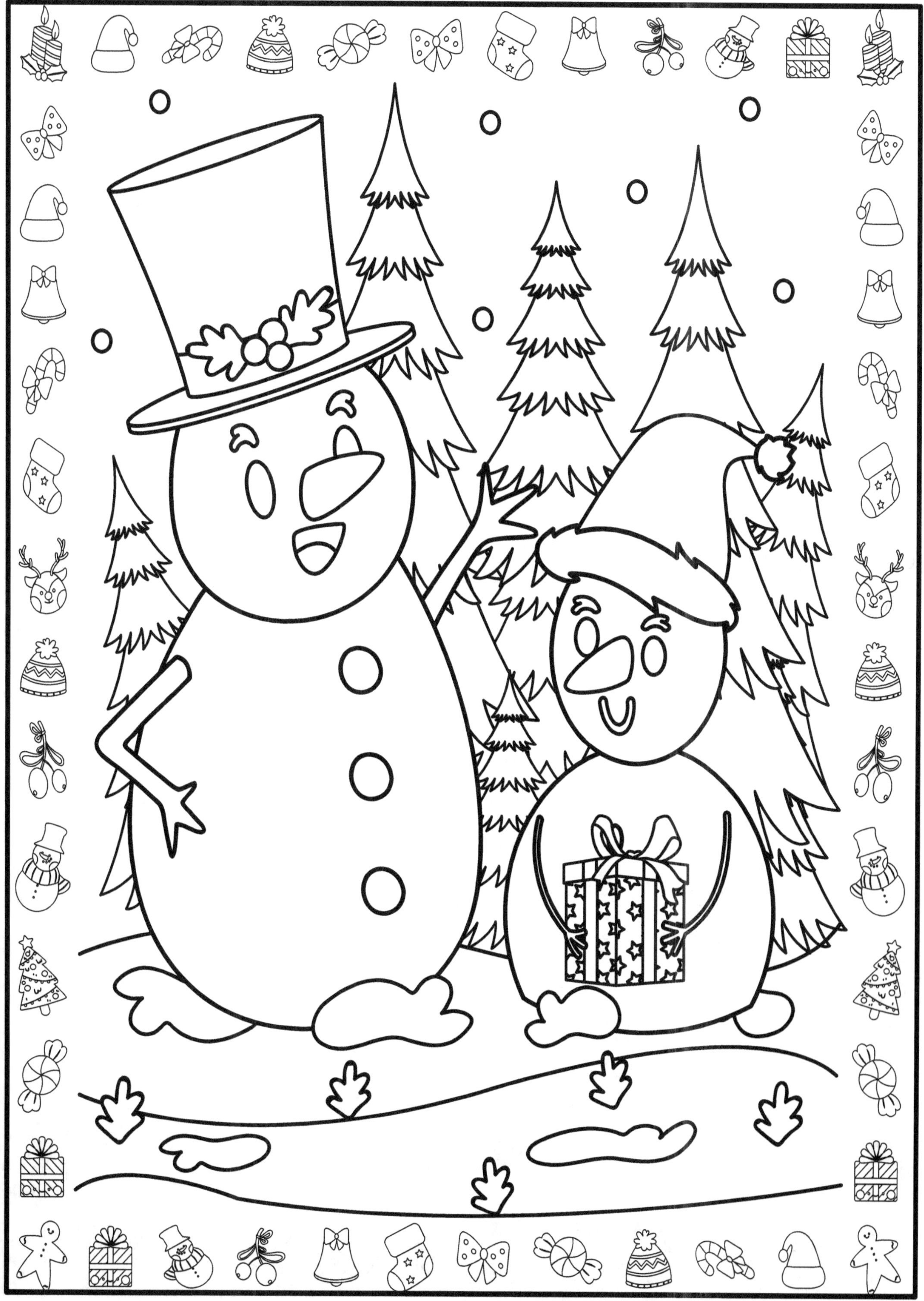

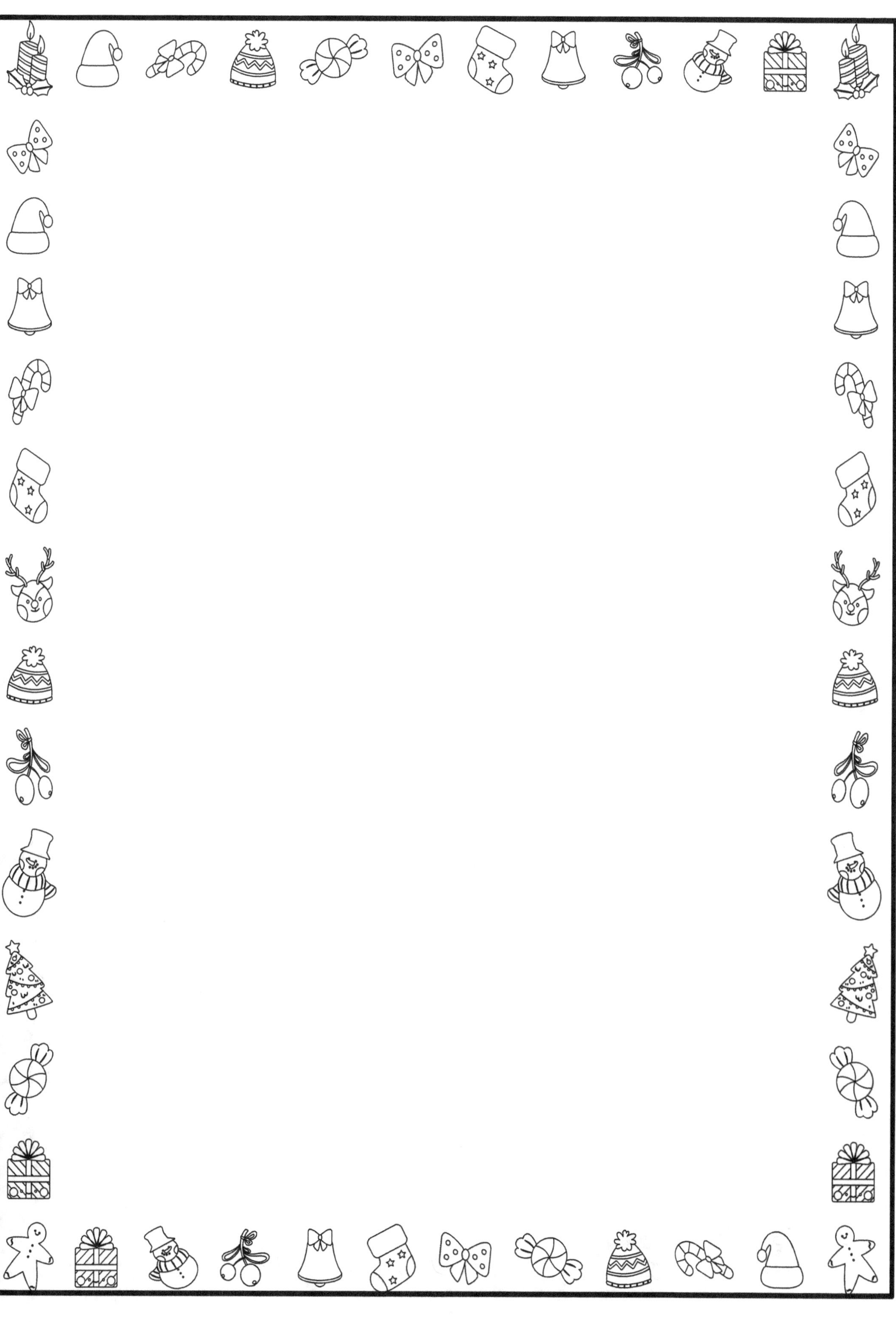

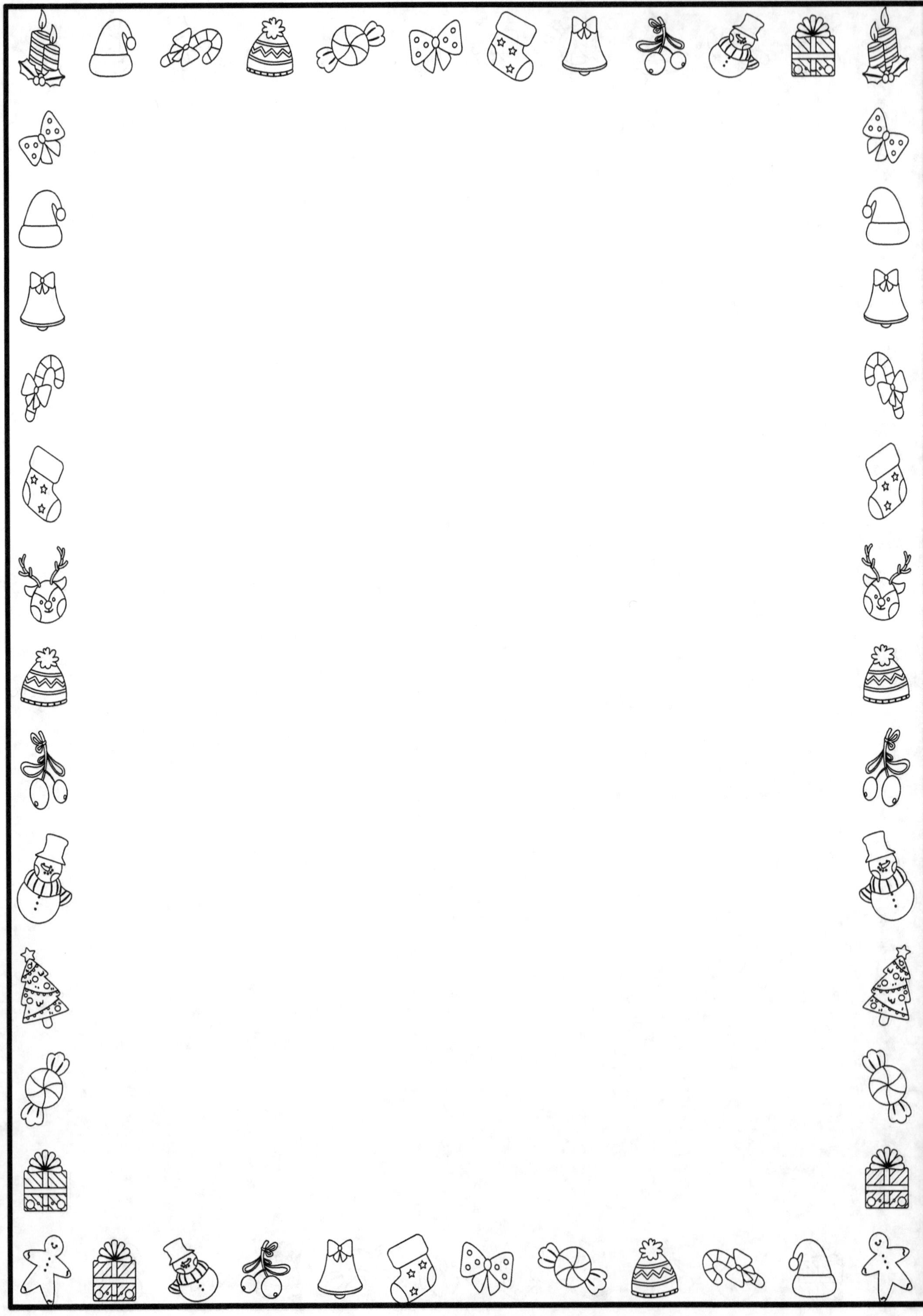

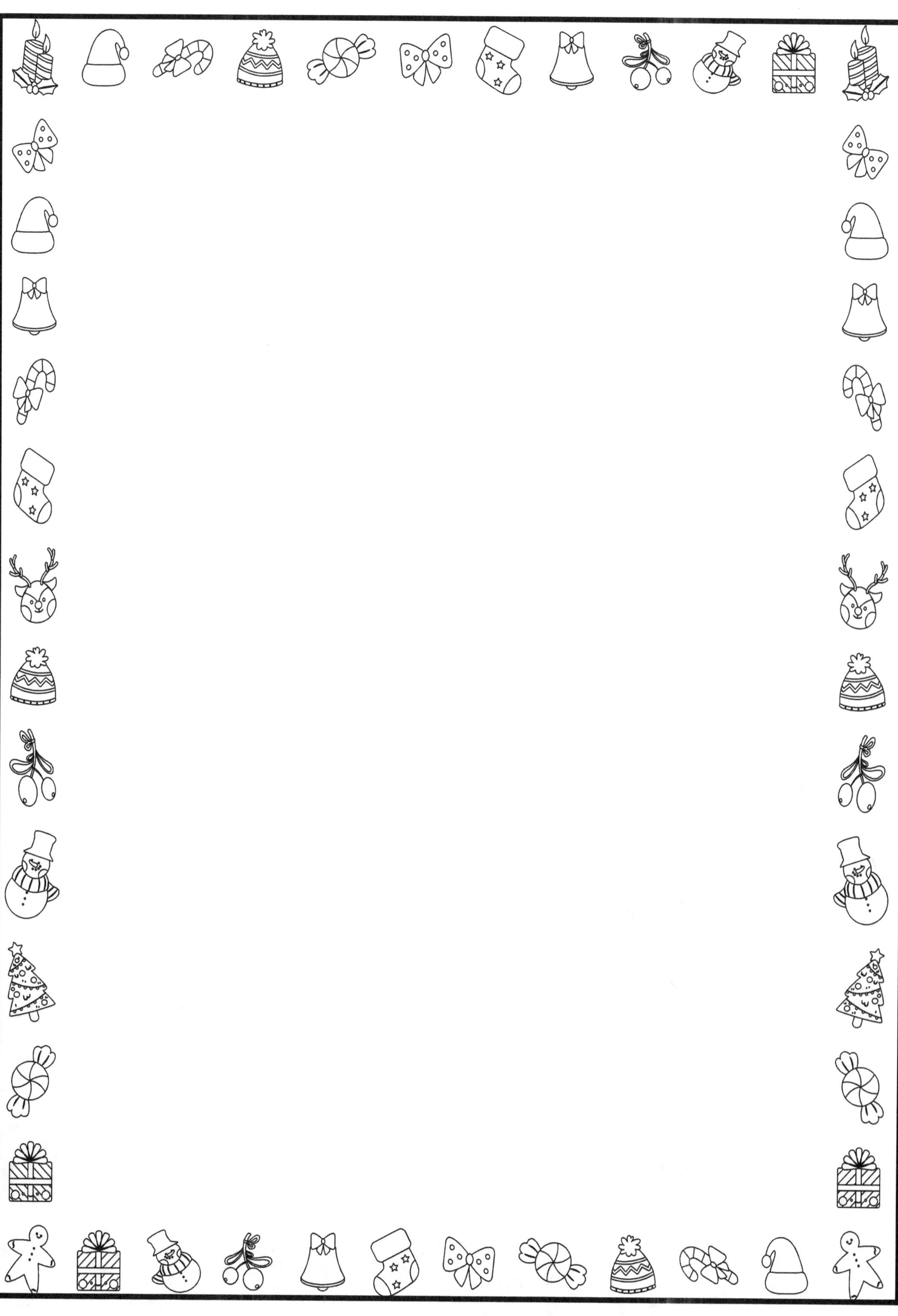

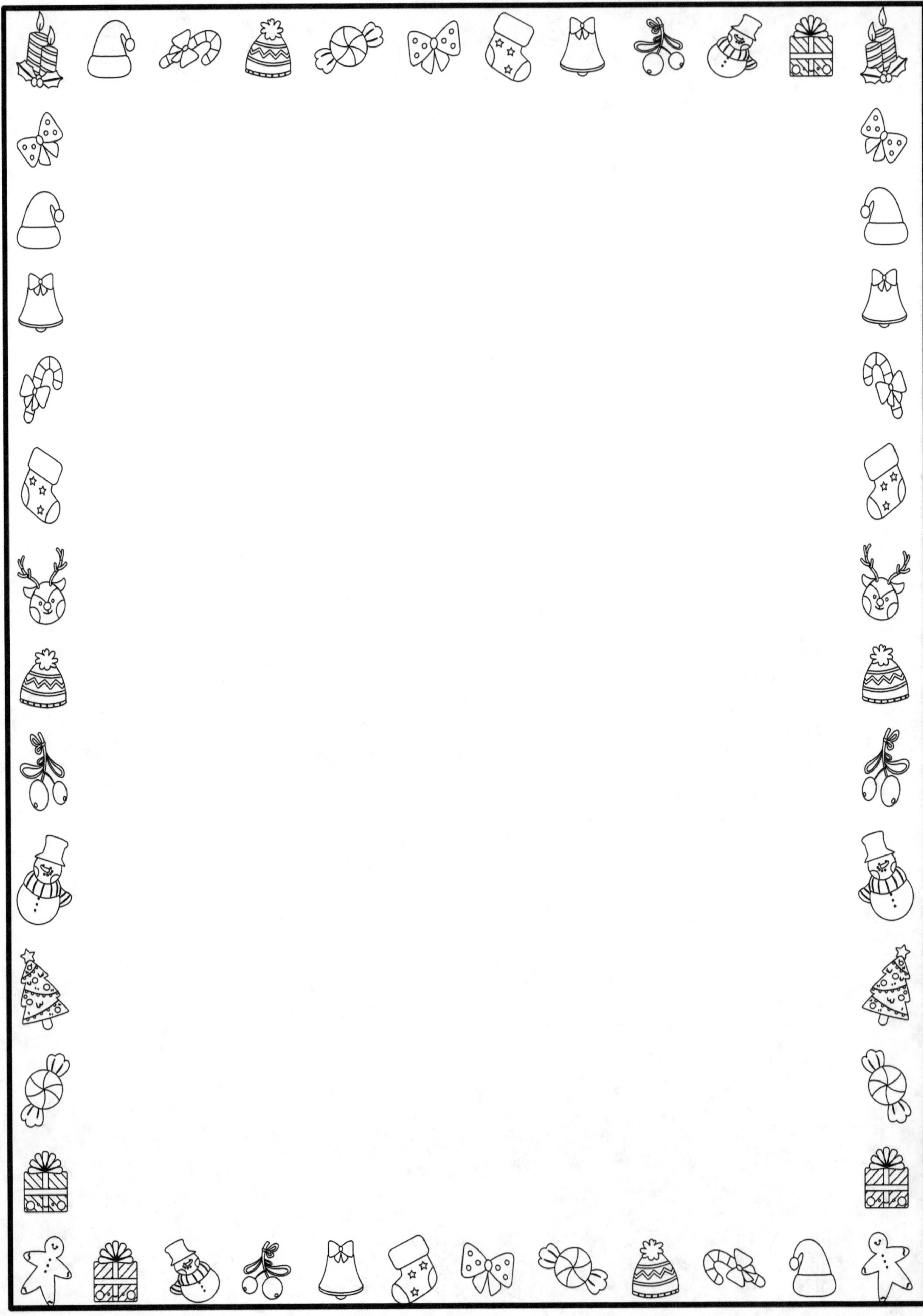